THE SEMINAR HANDBOOK...
AF333129
Increasing Student Spelling Achievement...
in daily writing across the curriculum
SPELLING STRATEGIES
REBECCA SITTON
EIGHTH EDITION

Dear Workshop Participant,

You are not alone. Teachers throughout the United States and Canada share your frustrations about students' spelling. I work with thousands of educators facing the spelling dilemma every year. They all tell me: Our kids can't spell even basic words in their writing! Some teachers faithfully use traditional spelling books...and their kids can't spell in their writing. Others have abandoned workbook spelling and use a system of their own, perhaps gathering words from across the curriculum. The result? Their students spell no better than those in spelling books! So, what to do?

Don't give in to spelling illiteracy...we are the gate-keepers of literacy and our kids need us...now, more than ever! Don't give up on spelling literacy...there is a light at the end of the tunnel shining brightly...we can see it now! That bright light is the incontestable agreement among parents, employers, teachers, school board members, everyone interested in basic literacy for today's children...that it's time to address spelling skills.

This is not to say we've failed at teaching spelling. I prefer to look at it this way. We've made terrific gains in our students' ability to write. Children are writing more and better than they did a decade ago. That's progress! And who gets credit for that progress! You do! But hand-in-hand with this progress came the revelation that too many of our students lack fundamental spelling skills. So, spelling is simply the missing puzzle piece for bringing the look for literacy to students' writing. And we can do it! We must...because we know how very important spelling is...misspellings quickly diminish the worth of a job application, a business or personal letter...as well as diminish the personal worth of the writer.

This seminar will open the door to practical options for creating a time-effective, cost-effective plan to improve your students' spelling literacy. None of the progress you've made in writing and language and literature-based instruction will be abandoned. We'll build on this base to create the foundation for spelling...the ABC's of spelling: accountability in writing, basic skills in spelling and related language concepts, and good old-fashioned common sense. A growing network of teachers are discovering new success with this sensible approach...you too can discover how to make it work for you...your way.

If you choose to apply the suggestions offered in the workshop, let me know your results. I want to hear from you! I want to help you with any challenges you have as you implement the ideas...and commend you for the progress you're sure to make. Please pass along to me any ideas you've discovered that may help others. Call or write me—my home phone number, FAX, and address are below...let's work together toward achieving basic spelling literacy for all our children. Every child a speller!

Sincerely,

Rebecca Sitton

South 2336 Pittsburg * Spokane, WA 99203
Phone: (509) 535-5500 * FAX: 509-533-9484

Rebecca Sitton is a free-lance Educational Consultant and author. Her focus is spelling literacy. She advocates a plan for the development of students' spelling accountability within their everyday writing across the curriculum and promotes the teaching of practical spelling skills with related language concepts. Her commonsense ideas are founded on research-based procedures and supported by thousands of educators across the United States and Canada who use her guidelines to develop their own spelling curriculums or to improve their existing programs.

She is an author of numerous language-integrated spelling, reading, and writing materials (see page 128) that complement writing-rich classrooms for preschool to adult education. You can read her articles in numerous educational publications, or read about her work in magazines and journals for teachers...see the article featuring a teacher using her spelling model in *LEARNING Magazine*, September 1995.

Rebecca has a spectrum of experiences in education...experienced classroom teacher in both regular and special education, school district language arts coordinator, staff development trainer, college instructor, and consultant to numerous school districts and regional education agencies.

She is a member of several education groups and frequently speaks on their behalf. This past year her conference calendar included Texas ASCD, Wisconsin Reading Association, California Reading Association, Western Regional IRA, and National IRA in New Orleans. Call her if you'd like her to speak at your conference.

Her fast-paced seminars offer an enormously practical, proven approach to the acquisition of fundamental spelling skills and concepts and their application in everyday writing...teachers of all experience levels find her seminars totally refreshing, with ideas that encourage a complete rethinking of spelling issues.

Christy Fong is a highly accomplished classroom teacher. Her classroom experience spans several years at various grade levels in both regular education and special education. The foundation for her career in education was initiated with a B.S. in Elementary Education from Weber State University with a Certificate in Learning Disabilities. This was followed by several years of classroom teaching while she completed her M. Ed. at Utah State University.

Christy considers herself a *teacher*...but, is now engaged in *teaching teachers* as a free-lance Educational Consultant. She was an outstanding SPELLING SOURCEBOOK Series user in her own classroom and now trains thousands of educators every year throughout the United States and Canada to use the options within Rebecca Sitton's methodology to bring spelling and language literacy to their students.

Using Rebecca Sitton's SPELLING SOURCEBOOK Series' guidelines, Christy Fong provides the framework through which educators can develop all the traditional spelling skills within a totally-integrated, language-based curriculum...bonded with *writing*. Her ideas...and the best ideas from her extensive network of teacher-users across the United States and Canada...provide educators with exciting and enormously sensible ideas for a successful spelling curriculum.

Christy's own experience becoming proficient with the SPELLING SOURCEBOOKS is invaluable to teachers who are just implementing the ideas and need the foundation, as well as the step-by-step, how-to suggestions to make them feel comfortable as new ground is forged. Her competence with the materials is also appreciated by the most experienced SOURCEBOOK users who are seeking those special ideas to refine and recharge their spelling instruction in the most productive ways.

The Video Series Training Guide for the SPELLING SOURCEBOOK videos was a recent project of Christy's. Her training manual is the new guide for the teacher-trainer to use to escort new teachers through the SPELLING SOURCEBOOK methodology of Video I "Introduction to Teachers" and Video III "Management & Record Keeping Options."

INTRODUCING BARBARA HANNO

Barbara Hanno is a free-lance Educational Consultant whose basic love is teaching. She has over three decades of professional teaching experiences. Her students have been people of all ages...kindergarten to the college level. She has taught people with various needs in a wide range of settings...from students in classrooms, teachers in schools, people in business, publishers in prominent publishing houses, and inmates in prisons. Her educational teaching has been extensive and diverse with awards that attest to her accomplishments, conscientiousness, and success within her profession.

She is a former classroom teacher with a background of teaching that includes working with students with severe learning challenges. As a school administrator, she guided teachers and expanded their instructional horizons resulting in documented school-wide results in significantly improved student performance. From this, she began teaching teachers across the United States and Canada to use effective teaching strategies with new language arts materials. Her concise seminars enabled teachers to comfortably and successfully implement programs that required changes in methods and materials. Then Barbara went on to teaching educational trainers...here she helped others develop state-of-the-art training programs that ensured success for teachers, students, and parents.

Barbara prepared for teaching at Montana State University where she earned a B. S. in Elementary Education. She received her M.A. degree in Education with emphasis on reading and language arts at Colorado State University. Beyond formal education, Barbara always stays abreast of educational trends and current thinking, but is founded in traditional, commonsense methodologies that afford learners the basic skills to think and grow for themselves.

Barbara and Rebecca Sitton have worked together on various educational projects spanning over twenty years. Their careers have consistently dovetailed. Now she works closely with Rebecca providing lively staff development for teachers using the SPELLING SOURCEBOOK methodology and assists Rebecca as new directions in education call for rethinking paradigms to ensure language literacy for students who must reflect skills to lead us through the challenges and changes for the years beyond 2000.

TABLE
of
CONTENTS

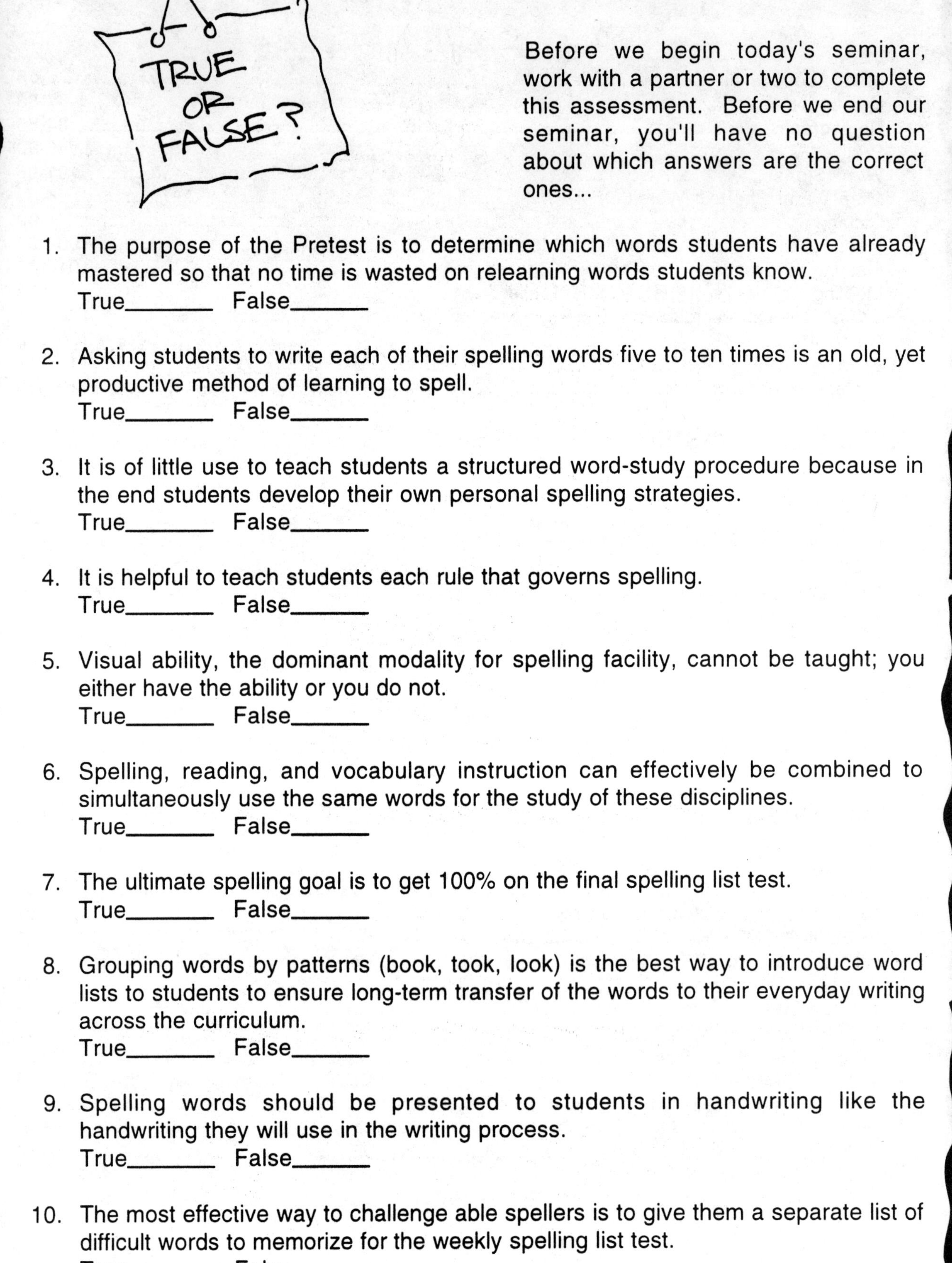

Before we begin today's seminar, work with a partner or two to complete this assessment. Before we end our seminar, you'll have no question about which answers are the correct ones...

1. The purpose of the Pretest is to determine which words students have already mastered so that no time is wasted on relearning words students know.
    True________   False________

2. Asking students to write each of their spelling words five to ten times is an old, yet productive method of learning to spell.
    True________   False________

3. It is of little use to teach students a structured word-study procedure because in the end students develop their own personal spelling strategies.
    True________   False________

4. It is helpful to teach students each rule that governs spelling.
    True________   False________

5. Visual ability, the dominant modality for spelling facility, cannot be taught; you either have the ability or you do not.
    True________   False________

6. Spelling, reading, and vocabulary instruction can effectively be combined to simultaneously use the same words for the study of these disciplines.
    True________   False________

7. The ultimate spelling goal is to get 100% on the final spelling list test.
    True________   False________

8. Grouping words by patterns (book, took, look) is the best way to introduce word lists to students to ensure long-term transfer of the words to their everyday writing across the curriculum.
    True________   False________

9. Spelling words should be presented to students in handwriting like the handwriting they will use in the writing process.
    True________   False________

10. The most effective way to challenge able spellers is to give them a separate list of difficult words to memorize for the weekly spelling list test.
    True________   False________

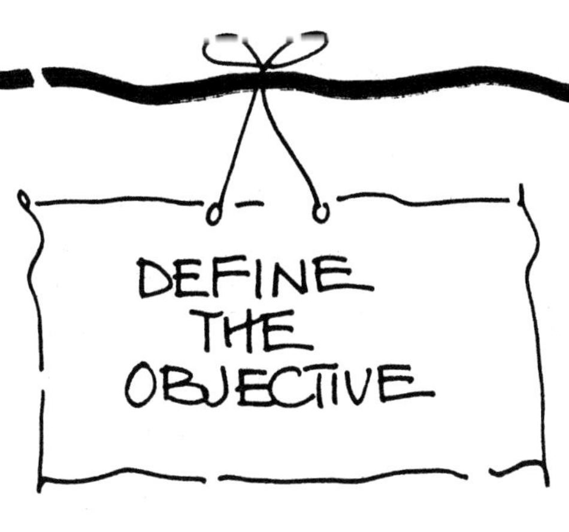

<u>What is our objective today?</u>

We want a spelling program that's going <u>to work</u>! When we look at our students' writing, we know there must be a better way. First, let's decide exactly what we want our spelling curriculum to accomplish...

There are two procedures that are supported strongly in the research...neither are new to you...

 the Independent-Word Study Procedure

 the Self-Corrected Test Procedure...or Pretest...or _______________

Removing the word "test" benefits three groups of students:

 Students who have exhibited a high anxiety level during traditional spelling tests often benefit by removing the word "test" because it reduces their anxiety level. This makes the procedure a far more productive study technique.

 Students who concentrate on fixing errors during the self-correction step often do so because they perceive the activity as a test. The procedure can be a more worthwhile study technique if students follow the guidelines, rather than focusing their attention on camouflaging mistakes.

 Students who spell all of the words correctly on a traditional spelling pretest may feel that they have "passed the test" and have no further obligation to these words. To avoid the misconception that the test has been passed at this point, the word "test" is best omitted. Spelling words in isolation does not demonstrate spelling mastery.

...and when are these procedures used?

 The Independent Word-Study procedure <u>is used anytime</u>...throughout a lifetime. It s steps are: Read, Spell, Cover, Print, Proofread. It is an effective alternative to the ineffective practice of having students write their words several times each.

 The Preview <u>is used to introduce a skill-building unit</u>.

 The Review <u>is used to close a skill-building unit</u>.

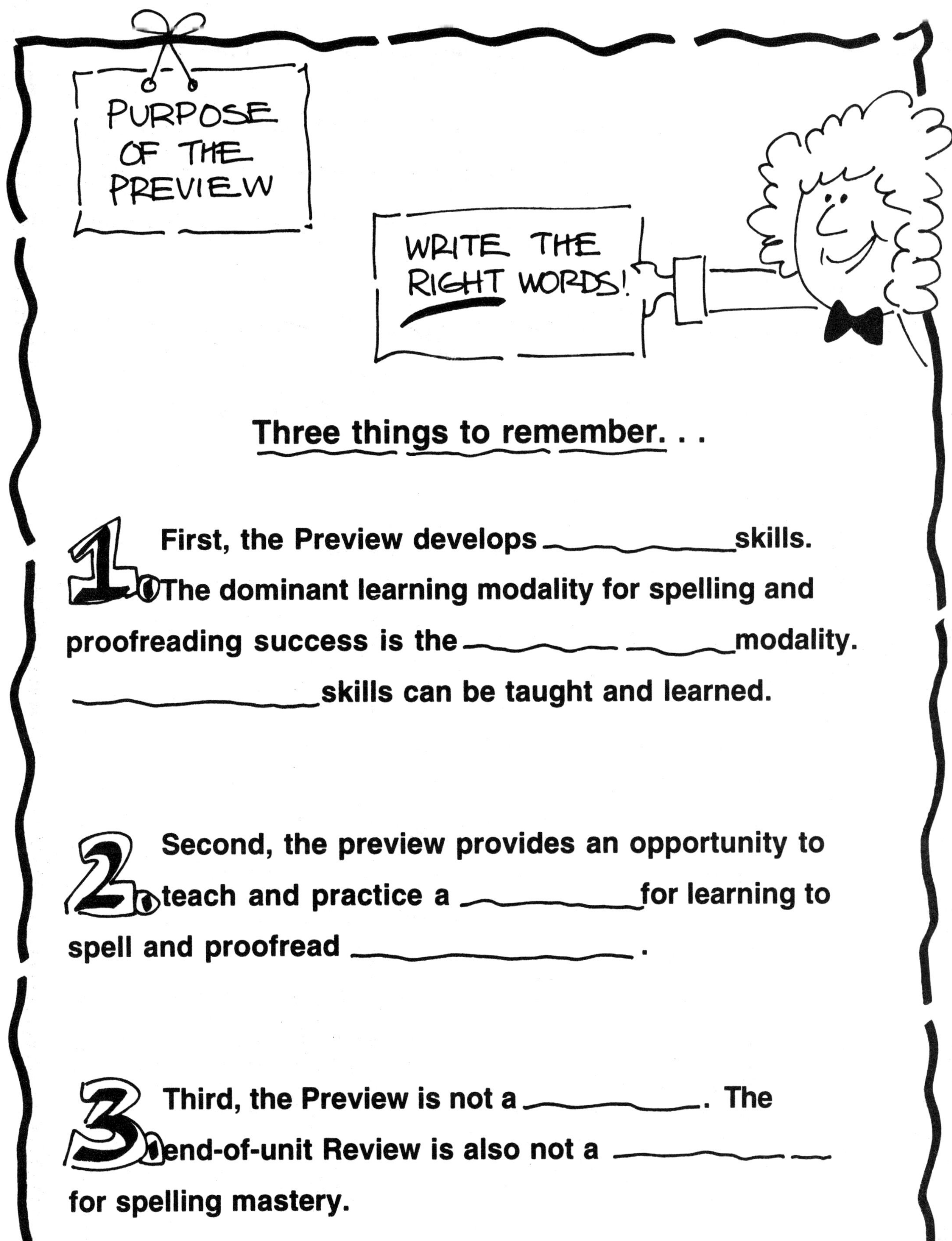

Three things to remember. . .

1. First, the Preview develops __________ skills. The dominant learning modality for spelling and proofreading success is the __________ __________ modality. __________ skills can be taught and learned.

2. Second, the preview provides an opportunity to teach and practice a __________ for learning to spell and proofread __________ .

3. Third, the Preview is not a __________ . The end-of-unit Review is also not a __________ for spelling mastery.

PRACTICE THE PREVIEW

Write

Rewrite

1.
2.
3.
4.
5.

1.
2.
3.
4.
5.

BLACKLINE MASTER FOR CLASSROOM USE...
PAGE 123

ADMINISTER...

TEACHER	STUDENTS
SAYS THE WORD. SAYS THE WORD IN A SENTENCE. SAYS THE WORD AGAIN.	LOOK AT THE TEACHER. LISTEN.
SIGNALS THE STUDENTS TO WRITE THE WORD.	PRINT THE WORD.

CORRECT...

TEACHER	STUDENTS
SPELLS THE WORD.	PROOFREAD THE WORD BY TOUCHING EACH LETTER WITH THE POINT OF A PENCIL. CIRCLE ERRORS.
PRINTS THE WORD ON THE BOARD AND SPELLS THE WORD ALOUD.	LOOK AT THE BOARD. LISTEN.
OBSERVES STUDENTS.	REWRITE THE WORD.

Does the Friday Test motivate your <u>top students</u> to reach the spelling goal?   YES   NO

Does the Friday Test motivate your <u>students challenged by spelling</u> to meet the spelling goal?   YES   NO

Is the Friday Test a <u>valid test</u> of spelling mastery?   YES   NO

Do you think every child deserves an <u>honorable chance</u> to be successful?   YES   NO

Would you like to <u>make it easier</u> for yourself and your students to reach the goal of spelling instruction?   YES   NO

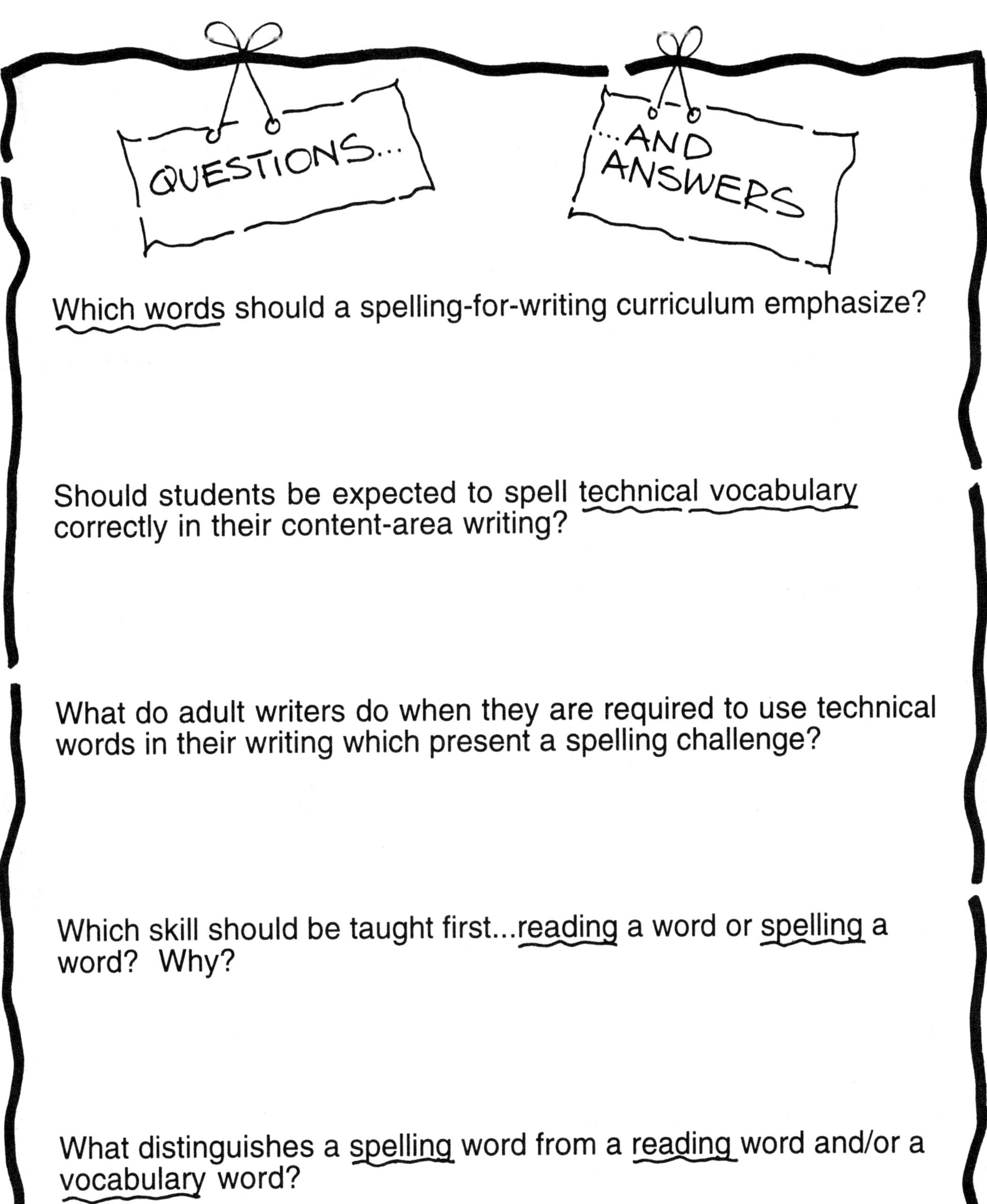

Which words should a spelling-for-writing curriculum emphasize?

Should students be expected to spell technical vocabulary correctly in their content-area writing?

What do adult writers do when they are required to use technical words in their writing which present a spelling challenge?

Which skill should be taught first...reading a word or spelling a word? Why?

What distinguishes a spelling word from a reading word and/or a vocabulary word?

SPELLING IS _______

____

____

____

SPELLING IS NOT _______

____

____

____

HIGH-FREQUENCY WORD RESEARCH
NUMBER OF WORDS
FREQUENCY OF USE
WHAT CHANGES WILL YOU MAKE IN LIGHT OF THIS RESEARCH?

THE HIGHEST-FREQUENCY WRITING WORDS

1.
2.
3.
4.
5.
6.
7.
8.
9.
10.
11.
12.
13.
14.
15.
16.
17.
18.
19.
20.

GET READY FOR A QUESTION !

What are the most frequently misspelled or misused words?

DEMONS

1. _______________
2. _______________
3. _______________
4. _______________
5. _______________
6. _______________
7. _______________

Remember...

...what is assessed establishes the <u>REAL</u> learning goal. What is assessed <u>BECOMES</u> the curriculum. And a conscientious curriculum is <u>AUTHENTIC</u>. It provides students with the skills they'll need for <u>SUCCESS</u> in the real world.

PARENT SUPPORT
1.
2.
3.
4.
5.
6.
7.
8.
PARENTS WILL BE YOUR BEST SUPPORTERS !

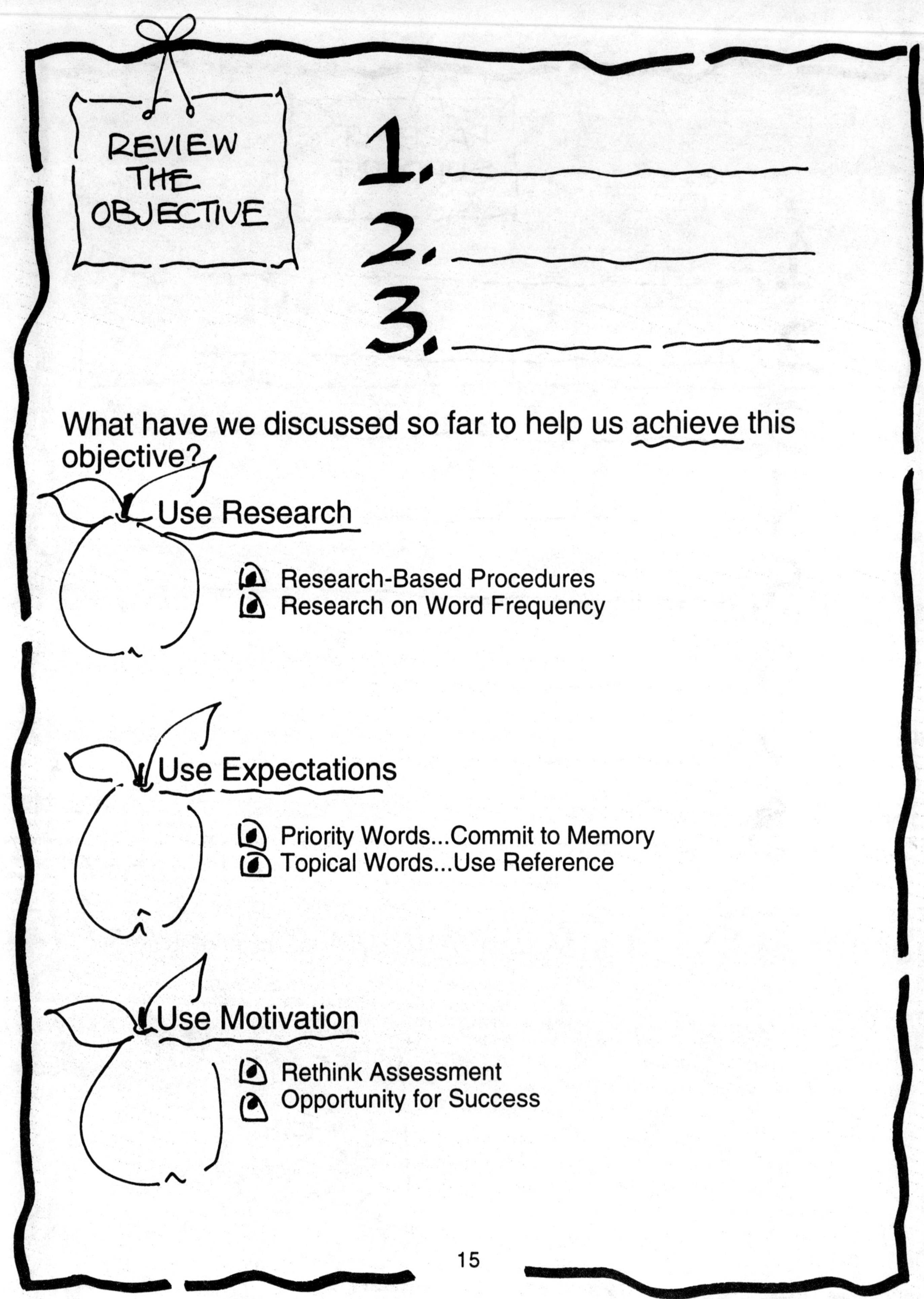
REVIEW THE OBJECTIVE

1.
2.
3.

What have we discussed so far to help us achieve this objective?

Use Research

Research-Based Procedures
Research on Word Frequency

Use Expectations

Priority Words...Commit to Memory
Topical Words...Use Reference

Use Motivation

Rethink Assessment
Opportunity for Success

PHONICS	PATTERNS	RULES	HOMOPHONES
play	bright	city	wait
train	sight	cities	weight
game	light	lady	here
		ladies	hear

In a traditional spelling program, the Word Lists tried to serve 2 purposes...

Why didn't students master the words?

Too many _______________

Too little _______________

Mastery was defined as _______________ .

DEVELOPING WORDS FOR TEACHING BASIC SKILLS

Which words do I use for teaching basic skills?

USE ________________ WORDS LISTED IN ORDER OF FREQUENCY OF USE. (SEE SOURCEBOOK 1 FOR A LIST OF 1200 WORDS.)

How should I divide the words by grade level?

#1 ________________ #1200

What guidelines should I follow for organizing the words?

FOR FIRST GRADE ________________ ________________.

FOR OTHER GRADES ________________ ________________.

What do we call this new bank of words?

THESE WORDS ARE THE ________________.

What purpose do these words serve?

THESE WORDS DEVELOP ________________, PLUS MORE!

1. PHONICS	2. PATTERNS	3. SPELLING RULES	4. HOMOPHONES	5. HOMOGRAPHS
6. ANTONYMS	7. SYNONYMS	8. OTHER WORD FORMS	9. COMPOUND WORDS	10. DOUBLE LETTERS
11. PALINDROMES	12. IDIOMS AND PROVERBS	13. THINKING SKILLS	14. WORD THEMES	15. RESEARCH
16. WORD ANALYSIS	17. WRITING	18. WORD ORIGINS	19. SHORT-CUT WORDS	20. BOOK TIE-INS
21. STUDY SKILLS	22. DICTATION	23. OFTEN-CONFUSED WORDS	24. MULTIPLE MEANINGS	25. CONTENT LEARNING
26. SPELLING GAMES	27. VISUAL SKILLS	28. USAGE AND GRAMMAR	29. PUBLIC SPEAKING	30. LIFE-SKILL RESOURCES

As the Core Words are introduced in their order of frequency of use, hundreds of additional words can be presented through the Springboard Activities. These additional words are Springboard Words. The words and activities provide opportunities to extend learning through exposure and discussion of words, skills, and multiple language concepts across the curriculum.

Following is a sampling of skills and concepts that may be taught through Springboard Activities, why they are important, and a specific example of each. The examples are from SPELLING SOURCEBOOKS 2, 3, and 4 (see section on <u>Rebecca Sitton's Materials</u>) which list all words with frequencies 1-1200 with a wide selection of activity ideas for each word.

1.   <u>Sound-Symbol Awareness</u>

A knowledge of phonics is a powerful aid to effective spelling. But, English spelling is not a perfectly phonetic system in which each letter consistently represents one sound. So, spelling cannot be learned solely through phonics. Nonetheless, the most reliable phonetic options for letters and letter combinations is an important aid to the able speller.

Example: (SPELLING SOURCEBOOK 2, word 272—*point*, page 94)
In this SOURCEBOOK activity, students find and write words that include the vowel sound that follows the *p* in *point*. Then students sort the words. They can be sorted into two reliable spelling categories—*oi* and *oy*. Students conclude that the *oi* is more prevalent for the sound and that the sound is always spelled *oy* at the end of a word.

2.   <u>Patterns</u>

Students can benefit from learning to observe spelling patterns among words. Pattern study can begin in the primary grades, but should continue as a powerful spelling aid into more sophisticated letter patterns.

Example: (SPELLING SOURCEBOOK 2, word 9—*that*, page 9) Students write new words from ___at (bat, sat, rat, etc.). Next, they write rhymes using the patterned rhyming words. Then they read them chorally. Many related language skills are interwoven.

Example: (SPELLING SOURCEBOOK 4, word 1126—*success*, page 114)
Students underline and observe the *ceed* suffix, meaning "go." They learn that other forms of the *ceed* suffix are *cede* and *sede*. They discover that only four words do not use the *cede* suffix: *succeed, exceed, proceed,* and *supersede*. All others use *cede*. Then students note the specific letter pattern in the suffix of these words and explore the words' meanings—*succeed, proceed, exceed, intercede, precede, concede, recede, accede, supersede*.

PAGES
61 - 65

... MORE ACTIVITIES!

3.   **Spelling Rules**

Some spelling rules apply to a large number of words, have few exceptions, and are easy to remember. These rules are worth teaching, as many writers can be aided by a knowledge of these few basic rules. When a Core Word illustrates one of these rules, it can be the agent to explore many words that follow the same rule.

PAGE 66

> **Example:** (SPELLING SOURCEBOOK 4, word 957—*valley*, page 58)
> Students write *valley* and examine the spelling rule for making plurals of nouns ending in vowel-y. Then they contrast this rule with the rule for making plurals of nouns ending in consonant-y. Students find and write multiple examples of words that follow these two basic rules.

4.   **Homophones**

Students may be given a homophone reference that uses tricky homophones in context sentences, such as the QUICK-WORD HANDBOOK (see section on <u>Rebecca Sitton's Materials</u>). Further, a large classroom chart can feature context sentences for those homophones that are persistently misused. Then, homophone mastery can be achieved through ongoing activities that cause students to use their homophone references as they write.

PAGES 67-83

> **Example:** (SPELLING SOURCEBOOK 2, word 134—*here*, page 48)
> Students complete a ready-made cloze activity with *here* and they review homophones *hear, there, their,* and the word *they're.* Then they are asked to make an inference regarding a solution to a problem posed through the cloze sentences and write their answer.

5.   **Homographs**

Usage, pronunciation, and word meanings can be reinforced as students encounter a Core Word that is a homograph.

PAGES 84-85

> **Example:** (SPELLING SOURCEBOOK 4, word 1172—*project*, page 128)
> Students check a dictionary for the different meanings and pronunciations of the homograph *project.* Then they are engaged in a timed-write game quickly listing homographs from memory with one point awarded for each correctly spelled homograph listed. Choices listed for teacher reference include these previously introduced Core Word homographs: *use, does, read, live, close, wind, present, object, minute, record, subject, produce, lead, row, separate, address, progress.*

6.   **Antonyms**

A vocabulary building activity can be created by springboarding from a Core Word to its antonym.

> **Example:** (SPELLING SOURCEBOOK 3, word 429—*beautiful*, page 18)
> Students identify the antonym of *beautiful*, the word *ugly.* Then they find two versions of "The Ugly Duckling," compare and contrast them, then write their own version.

7. **Synonyms**

To further develop students' vocabulary skills, synonyms of the Core Words can be explored.

> **Example:** (SPELLING SOURCEBOOK 3, word 468—*walked*, page 30)
> In this activity, students explore synonyms for *walk*, such as *amble, lumber, meander, plod, prance, saunter, shuffle, stagger, stroll, strut, swagger, totter, trek, trudge*. After discussing the words' meanings, students write a description of a story character or real person who is walking in one of these special ways.

8. **Other Word Forms**

A basic word-building activity for students who need a challenge is to work with word forms. Large charts can be posted of often-used suffixes and often-used prefixes. Then ask students to determine and write the other word forms for each Core Word.

> **Example:** (SPELLING SOURCEBOOK 4, word 972—*population*, page 63)
> In this activity that focuses on suffixes, students are asked to brainstorm for common other word forms of *population: populations, populate, populates, populated, populating, populace, populous*. Unfamiliar words are discussed. Then students write these questions with answers to integrate spelling, vocabulary development, writing, and social studies:
>> What is the population of your state or province?
>> Where is the populace concentrated? Why?

> **Example:** (SPELLING SOURCEBOOK 2, word 270—*turned*, page 94)
> In this activity that springboards from the Core Word *turned*, students answer questions that highlight review Core Words with the re prefix. The questions include:
>> What would happen if you <u>returned</u> your library book after the due date?
>> Why might it be necessary to <u>restudy</u> information for a test?
>> What book would you like to <u>reread</u>? Why?
>> What things does your family <u>reuse</u>?
>> What might you choose to <u>rename</u> your school?

9. **Compound Words**

A visual instructional focus on compounds helps students see words in words to make the spelling of multi-letter compounds surprisingly easy for students. Activities can either focus on the analysis of compounds to make them into two easy words, or they can synthesize compounds by making two known words into a compound.

> **Example:** (SPELLING SOURCEBOOK 3, word 578—*eye*, page 66)
> In this activity, the easy-to-spell *eye* becomes the agent for learning compounds that use *eye*. Students find and write compound words that use

eye: eyeball, eyelash, eyebrow, eyelid, eyedropper, eyesight, eyewitness. After they have discussed unfamiliar words, they write an eyewitness account of a real or make-believe happening.

10. Double Letters

Double letters never create a reading problem, but do present a persistent spelling challenge. Visual activities that note double letters are necessary to meet this challenge.

Example: (SPELLING SOURCEBOOK 4, word 1084—*coffee*, page 100) Students write and underline the two sets of double letters in *coffee, address, accidentally, success, accommodate, embarrassed, misspell, possess, occasionally, mattress.* Then they find and write more examples of words with two sets of double letters—then three sets of double letters, such as *bookkeeper, committee, successfully, Mississippi.*

11. Palindromes

Words, phrases, and sentences that are spelled the same forwards and backwards are called palindromes. Students who have no dyslexic tendencies like the challenge of identifying palindromes.

Example: (SPELLING SOURCEBOOK 3, page 734—*level*, page 116) Students examine *level* as a palindrome. Then they find and write more palindromes, such as *mom, pop, noon, level, deed, peep, did, eve, Bob, Anna, Nan, radar, madam, tot, toot, kayak, repaper, rotator, eye.* The activity identifies these palindrome sentences for students to ponder: *Step on no pets, Was it a car or a cat I saw?, Pull up if I pull up.*

12. Idioms and Proverbs

All students, and particularly those for which English is their second language, can learn how meaning transcends a Core Word when idioms and proverbs are discussed.

Example: (SPELLING SOURCEBOOK 3, word 600—*speak*, page 73) Students explain in writing what they think it means to say these expressions and then each is discussed:

Actions *speak* louder than words.	to *speak* your mind
nothing to *speak* of	to *speak* out of turn
so to *speak*	to *speak* up

13. Thinking Skills

Students can practice thinking skills as they engage in sequencing, analogies, and sorting exercises. Through the writing activities they practice thinking skills including hypothesizing, explaining, comparing and contrasting, generalizing, judging, and making inferences. Word games challenge students to seek out solutions through logic, meaning, and word relationships. The possibilities are endless!

Example: (SPELLING SOURCEBOOK 4, word 1200—*recommend*, page 137)

In this recurring activity, students learn to observe words and think logically about their relationships. They write the words in the rows, choose one that does not belong, and write why it is different from the others, such as:

1. recommend * tomorrow * community * swimming * immediately
2. waste * affect * message * peace * die
3. improve * suggest * advise * propose * recommend

More than one answer can be correct, but #1 might be *tomorrow* because it has only one *m*—a point worth reinforcing; #2 might be *message* because it is not a homophone; and #3 could be *improve* because the other words are synonyms for one another.

14. <u>**Word Themes**</u>

A Core Word can be a catalyst for students to brainstorm for related words. This can build spelling skills, related language skills, and new word relationships.

Example: (SPELLING SOURCEBOOK 3, word 501—*music*, page 41)

The theme for the word bank that students create in this activity stems from the book *The Philharmonic Gets Dressed* (Karla Kuskin, Harper) which focuses on the preparation of orchestra members for a performance. Students identify and write the names of musical instruments pictured in the book.

15. <u>**Research**</u>

Developing the study skills of finding, recording, and reporting information is exciting to develop through Core Words.

Example: (SPELLING SOURCEBOOK 3, word 611—*record*, page 76)

In this activity, students research animal *records*...the biggest fish (whale shark), the biggest animal (blue whale), the biggest land mammal (African elephant), the biggest reptile (colossal saltwater crocodile), the tallest animal (giraffe), the smallest bird (hummingbird), the animal that can jump the highest (puma), the fastest land mammal (cheetah), the fastest animal (peregrine falcon), the longest-lived animal (tortoise). Of course, a book reference is provided in which the information could be found.

16. <u>**Word Analysis**</u>

Words can be analyzed for a variety of reasons, such as phonetically, structurally, or for meaning and usage. Students grow in their word awareness as they are given opportunities to observe words for different reasons.

Example: (SPELLING SOURCEBOOK 4, word 1162—*cancel*, page 125)

Students explore the variant spellings of British and American English as they make *cancel* into *canceled* and *canceling* (or the British spellings, *cancelled*, *cancelling*). Then they analyze *traveler/traveller, leveled/levelled, jewelry/jewellry, woolen/woollen.* The lesson is extended to many American/British spelling variations and the letter-group options that spell each.

17. Writing

Most of the Springboard Activities engage students in writing. Students write lists, journal entries, explanations, greeting cards, letters, news stories, reliable spelling rules, posters, announcements, telephone messages, riddles, jokes, advertisements, summaries, descriptions, book reviews, directions, similes, dialogues, lyrics, opinions, story sequels, epitaphs, fables, tall tales, poetry, menus, books, brochures, etc.

Example: (SPELLING SOURCEBOOK 2, word 225—*year*, page 79)
This lesson is introduced with *Farm Boy's Year* (David McPhail, Atheneum) which uses journal entries to tell about a late nineteenth century New England boy's daily life. After the reading, students begin a daily journal that highlights their everyday life.

18. Word Origins

A genuine interest in words can often be cultivated through word origins. For example, the computer industry has generated many new exciting words. Some words have been borrowed from other languages or from people/place names (eponyms). As students explore word origins, their understanding of their language grows.

Example: (SPELLING SOURCEBOOK 4, word 813—*bread*, page 31)
This activity provides an opportunity for students to research the origin of the eponym *sandwich*. The Fourth Earl of Sandwich asked his servants to bring him meat between two pieces of *bread*. The lesson is extended to students researching the eponymous origins of *saxophone, levis, teddy bear, Graham crackers, guppies, diesel, and bikini.* Of course, a book is suggested in which the answers can all be found.

PAGES
91-95

19. Short-Cut Words

Writers and speakers take legal shortcuts. We use contractions (I'd), initializations (TV), abbreviations (pd.), acronyms (ZIP code), clipped words (plane/airplane), blends (brunch). Students can extend their understanding of words and their spellings through a study of short-cut words.

Example: (SPELLING SOURCEBOOK 4, word 1038—*bicycle*, page 86)
In this activity, students review clipped words, such as the review Core Word *plane* (airplane). Then they find and write more clipped words. Clipped words provided for teacher reference in this activity are *auto/automobile, sis/sister, mart/market, phone/telephone, sub/submarine, champ/champion, ref/referee, math/mathematics, gym/ gymnasium, limo/limousine, gas/gasoline, teen/teenager.*

PAGES
96-99

20. Book Tie-Ins

Literature is a powerful catalyst for writing. Use books to introduce a topic related to a Core Word with a writing follow-up activity.

Example: (SPELLING SOURCEBOOK 2, word 298—*red*, page 102)
A variation of the popular Red Riding Hood tale, *Lon Po Po: A Red-Riding Hood Story from China* (Ed Young, Philomel), is introduced to students. Then they compare and contrast this and other versions to highlight similarities and differences.

Example: (SPELLING SOURCEBOOK 4, word 1180—*courage*, page 131)
In this activity, students research books that share the lives of people who have displayed courage. *Rosa Parks: My Story* (Rosa Parks and Jim Haskins, Dial), is suggested as an example. It recounts the events of 1955 when Parks challenged existing segregation laws. As a follow-up writing project, students create a bibliography of books about courageous people with a brief description of each. Then students sign their name to the bibliography when they complete reading one of the books cited.

21. **Study Skills**

The most capable students have developed the facility for using study skills across the curriculum. Often a Core Word can be the agent to practice study skills.

Example: (SPELLING SOURCEBOOK 4, word 1062—*chapter*, page 94)
The word *chapter* provides an opportunity to explore the organization of a book. A content-area text is selected. Students see what they can learn from the title page, copyright page, the table of contents, the glossary, and index. Then teacher-made copies of several table of contents pages from chapter books that are unfamiliar to students provide students with the task of determining what can be learned about the organization and content of the books solely from these pages. Students write their perceptions and predictions.

22. **Dictation**

Dictation provides practice for spelling as well as many related language skills. If teachers like to use dictation, it can be accommodated through the Springboard Activities. Through the dictation, other concepts and/or skills can be reinforced.

Example: (SPELLING SOURCEBOOK 4, word 1173—*pronounce*, page 129)
This open-ended dictation uses review Core Words and their other word forms. It also reviews the correct pronunciation of *environment* and *government*, two previously introduced words that may be misspelled if they are mispronounced. *Correct pronunciation can help a writer avoid misspellings. For example, carefully pronouncing the words environment and government will make the words easier to spell. If they are pronounced properly, the writer won't forget...*

PAGE 100

23. **Often-Confused Words**

Homophones are often confused, but many words that simply look and/or sound alike are also challenging. Students need to review these often. When a word that may be confusing appears in the Core Word list, it provides the catalyst for reinforcing other persistently confusing word sets.

Example: (SPELLING SOURCEBOOK 3, word 726—*quiet*, page 113)
In this activity, *quiet* is contrasted with *quite* and *quit*. Then these word sets are discussed: *maybe* and *may be*, *already* and *all ready*, *our* and *are*, *then* and *than*, *picture* and *pitcher*. Of course, any other confusing sets of words could be added to the lesson. Students follow up by using each of the sets of words in sentences.

PAGES 103-104

24.   **Multiple Meanings**

The reason the high-frequency words are used more often than other words is because many of them have several different meanings. Students can explore the variant meanings and uses of these words as they learn to spell them.

Example: (SPELLING SOURCEBOOK 2, word 264—*change*, page 91)
The little housemaid, Amelia Bedelia, misinterprets the directions of her employers, Mr. and Mrs. Rogers, for some good chuckles and many interesting plays on words in a series of stories by Peggy Parish. Use them as a model for students to write their own silly Amelia scenarios. In this lesson, the students learn how Amelia "changes" the towels.

Example: (SPELLING SOURCEBOOK 4, word 956—*pound*, page 58)
Many lessons on multiple meanings take the format used in this lesson: Students explain in writing how a British banker, a carpenter, a dieter, and a veterinarian might use the word *pound* to mean something different.

25.   **Content Learning**

The spelling-writing-learning connection applies to all content areas. When a Core Word lends itself to a tie-in with another curriculum area, take advantage of the opportunity to teach both.

Example: (SPELLING SOURCEBOOK 3, word 539—*teacher*, page 53)
Students learn about career opportunities in which they would work within a school setting in this lesson, such as a *teacher*, principal, librarian, custodian, speech therapist, school nurse, food servicer, secretary...and the person who comes to fix the copy machine each week. Then they explore the skills necessary to do these jobs.

26.   **Games**

Spelling games are not a waste of time when they foster eager participation among students learning spelling and related skills.

Example: (SPELLING SOURCEBOOK 4, word 1090—*dictionary*, page 102)
In this lesson, students note the plural form of *dictionary* and then find more words that follow this spelling pattern. Then with their bank of words, they develop a crossword puzzle for a classmate to complete using graph paper or a blackline master grid.

PAGES 105-112

27. **<u>Visual Skills</u>**

The visual modality is the most important for spelling success. Fortunately, visual skills can be taught and learned. Throughout conscientious spelling instruction, visual skills need to be taught and practiced.

> **Example:** (SPELLING SOURCEBOOK 3, word 748—*love*, page 120)
> In the Word Look-Alike game, students look at words in rows and circle the words like the underlined word. Then they turn their paper over and write the underlined word from memory. One row of the game looks like this:
>> <u>love</u>   live   line   love   dove   glove   lone
>
> Next, students make their own Word Look-Alike games for a classmate to play.

28. **<u>Usage and Grammar Skills</u>**

Using conventional language, both orally and written, gives the user power. There are many opportunities to create connections between correct usage and grammar skills and spelling instruction.

> **Example:** (SPELLING SOURCEBOOK 4, word 801—*sell*, page 125)
> When "easy" words appear in the Core Word continuum, don't diminish their importance as a catalyst for related learning. For example, the word *sell* becomes the agent for a lesson on irregular verb forms. Students note that the past tense of *sell* is not *selled*, but *sold*. Then they find and write more examples, such as *said, made, gave, built, lost, meant, won, wore, forgot*.

29. **<u>Public Speaking</u>**

One situation feared by many adults is speaking publicly. As students learn to use language, they can ease into skills that will diminish this fear. The spelling curriculum and public speaking can be united to develop confident public speakers.

> **Example:** (SPELLING SOURCEBOOK 2, word 307—*book*, page 106)
> In this lesson, students find and write information on Caldecott and Newbery Medal *books*, the most popular children's *books*, and/or the career of a book *editor*. Then they prepare the information to present orally to the class.

30. **<u>Using Everyday Lifeskill Resources</u>**

As students explore the related-learning opportunities presented with the Core Words, one recurring skill is the use of resources, such as a dictionary, thesaurus, encyclopedia, telephone directory, almanac, timetable, newspaper, and map.

> **Example:** (SPELLING SOURCEBOOK 4, word 1068—*telephone*, page 95)
> In this activity, students use the yellow pages of a *telephone* directory. They write the listing category they would consult for finding out these things: where to buy toys and games for use in a swimming pool, where to get a cost estimate for a new mountain bike, where to trade basketball cards, where to get your winter coat altered, where to get your team name monogrammed on your baseball cap, where to get trail maps for hiking, where to rent a guitar, where to find a Korean restaurant, where the closest laundromat is located, and where to get a waterbed repaired.

SPRINGBOARD ACTIVITIES PROVIDE....

1.
2.
3.
4.
5.
6.
7.

HOW IS CAREFUL REVIEW ACHIEVED ?

1. What is the purpose of a Core Word?

2. Why are some Core Words so easy?

3. Where do you begin teaching the Core Words?

4. How are Core Words introduced to students?

5. How many Core Words should be introduced at one time?

6. What is the time frame for teaching a unit of Core Words?

7. How is a unit brought to a close..is there a test?

8. What happens to the Core Words after a unit?

9. What is the difference between a Core Word and a Priority Word?

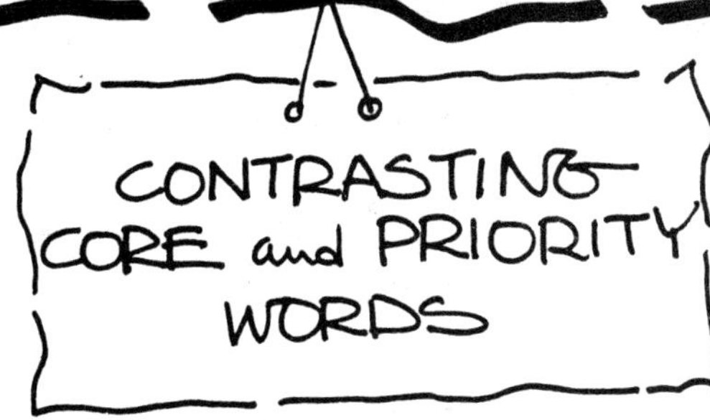

CORE...	PRIORITY...
Basic Skills	Accountability
Develop Spelling and Related Language Skills	Develop Proofreading Responsibility in Writing
General Growth	Specific Growth
A fixed list of grade-level words	A list that grows over time
Are complemented by Springboard Words	Are complemented by Topical Words
Practiced and Reinforced over time for continued <u>exposure</u>	Practiced and Reinforced over time through everyday writing to maintain <u>mastery</u>

To establish <u>accountability</u> for Priority Words in everyday writing...

1. <u>Identify</u> the Priority Words

2. <u>Provide</u> the words to students

3. State the <u>expectations</u>

4. Create opportunities for <u>everyday writing</u>

5. Furnish performance <u>feedback</u> from writing samples

6. Assess progress (<u>grading</u>)

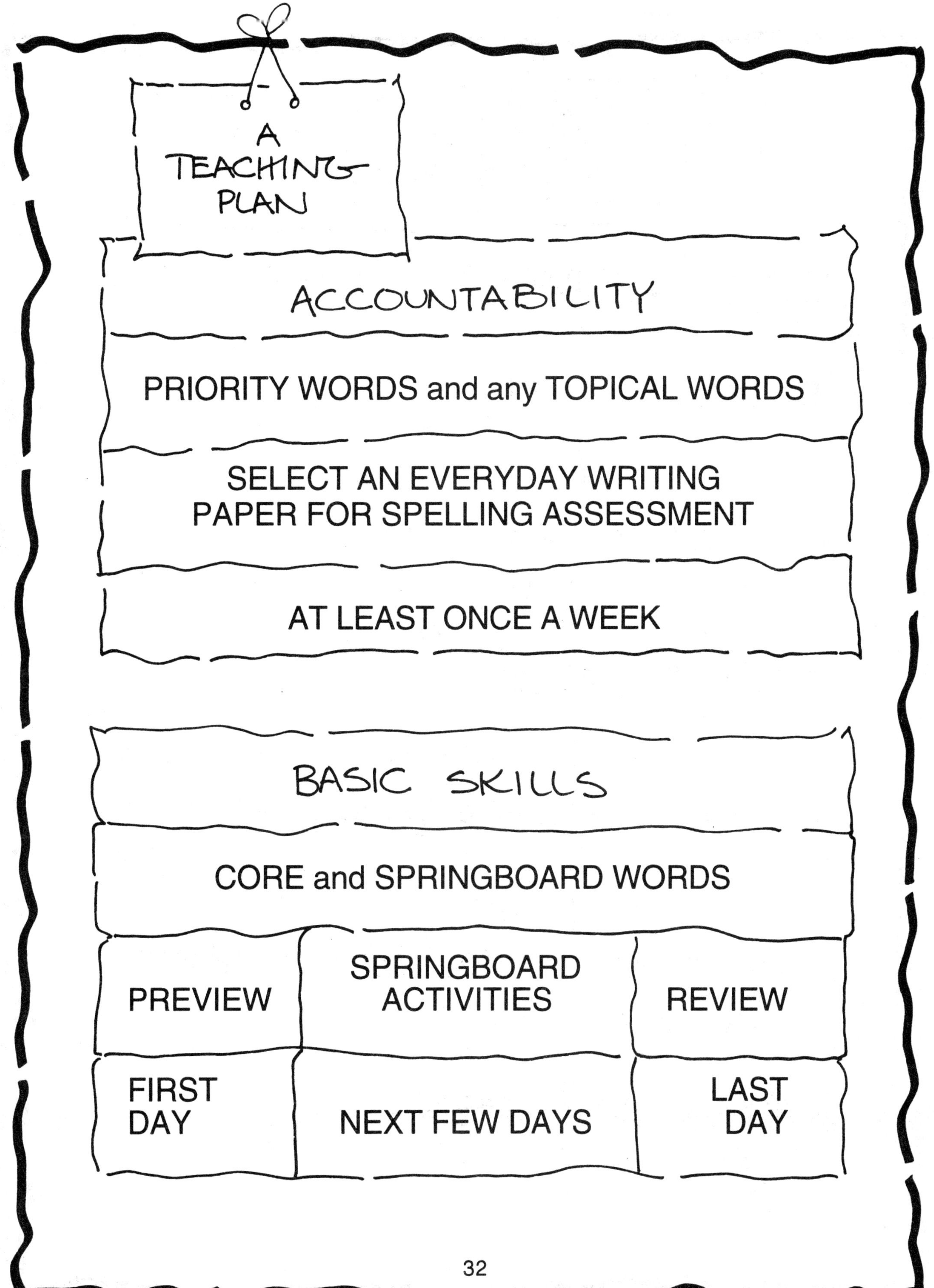

A TEACHING PLAN

ACCOUNTABILITY

PRIORITY WORDS and any TOPICAL WORDS

SELECT AN EVERYDAY WRITING
PAPER FOR SPELLING ASSESSMENT

AT LEAST ONCE A WEEK

BASIC SKILLS

CORE and SPRINGBOARD WORDS

PREVIEW
SPRINGBOARD
ACTIVITIES
REVIEW

FIRST
DAY
NEXT FEW DAYS
LAST
DAY

EXPANDING THE PROGRAM

WE MUST MEET A VARIETY OF NEEDS...

The individualized list...

Junior High - Middle School   WHAT TO DO?

Students with special spelling challenges

The capable speller

WHAT NEXT ?
So...there you have it ! What to do next ?
DEVELOP YOUR PLAN FOR SPELLING LITERACY !

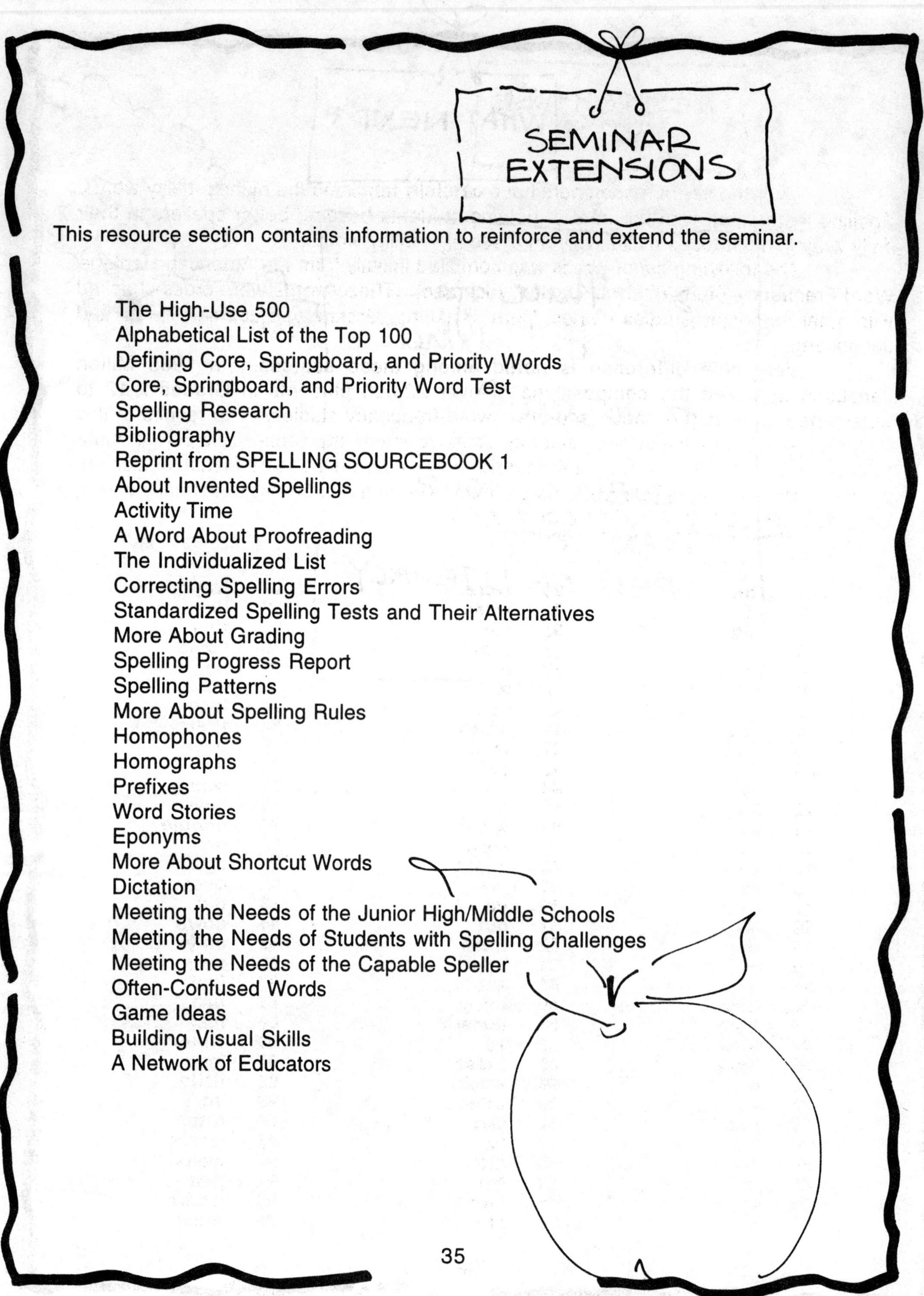

This resource section contains information to reinforce and extend the seminar.

THE HIGH-USE 500

Over the years researchers have carefully tabulated the highest-utility words. Spelling instruction, with the goal of helping students become better spellers in their daily writing, must focus exclusively on these high-utility words.

The following list of words was compiled initially from the American Heritage Word Frequency Study (Carroll, Davies, Richman). These words were cross-checked with other respected studies (Gates, Horn, Rinsland, Greene and Loomer, Harris and Jacobson).

Very little difference is noted among these sources. In 1985 Milton Jacobson analyzed the compositions of over 22,000 students in Grades 2-12 to determine the validity of these and other word-frequency studies. The results of this intensive analysis indicated that students continue to use the same basic core of high-frequency words in their writing and that the minor differences in frequency placement of words on the various lists were insignificant. (From the 1200 high-frequency writing word list, **SPELLING SOURCEBOOK 1**.)

1	the	34	were	67	him
2	of	35	when	68	see
3	and	36	we	69	time
4	a	37	there	70	could
5	to	38	can	71	no
6	in	39	an	72	make
7	is	40	your	73	than
8	you	41	which	74	first
9	that	42	their	75	been
10	it	43	said	76	its
11	he	44	if	77	who
12	for	45	do	78	now
13	was	46	will	79	people
14	on	47	each	80	my
15	are	48	about	81	made
16	as	49	how	82	over
17	with	50	up	83	did
18	his	51	out	84	down
19	they	52	them	85	only
20	at	53	then	86	way
21	be	54	she	87	find
22	this	55	many	88	use
23	from	56	some	89	may
24	I	57	so	90	water
25	have	58	these	91	long
26	or	59	would	92	little
27	by	60	other	93	very
28	one	61	into	94	after
29	had	62	has	95	words
30	not	63	more	96	called
31	but	64	her	97	just
32	what	65	two	98	where
33	all	66	like	99	most

(From the 1200 high-frequency writing word list, **SPELLING SOURCEBOOK 1**.)

100	know	150	small	200	children
101	get	151	every	201	feet
102	through	152	found	202	land
103	back	153	still	203	side
104	much	154	between	204	without
105	go	155	name	205	boy
106	good	156	should	206	once
107	new	157	home	207	animal
108	write	158	big	208	life
109	our	159	give	209	enough
110	me	160	air	210	took
111	man	161	line	211	four
112	too	162	set	212	head
113	any	163	own	213	above
114	day	164	under	214	kind
115	same	165	read	215	began
116	right	166	last	216	almost
117	look	167	never	217	live
118	think	168	us	218	page
119	also	169	left	219	got
120	around	170	end	220	earth
121	another	171	along	221	need
122	came	172	while	222	far
123	come	173	might	223	hand
124	work	174	next	224	high
125	three	175	sound	225	year
126	must	176	below	226	mother
127	because	177	saw	227	light
128	does	178	something	228	country
129	part	179	thought	229	father
130	even	180	both	230	let
131	place	181	few	231	night
132	well	182	those	232	picture
133	such	183	always	233	being
134	here	184	show	234	study
135	take	185	large	235	second
136	why	186	often	236	soon
137	help	187	together	237	story
138	put	188	asked	238	since
139	different	189	house	239	white
140	away	190	don't	240	ever
141	again	191	world	241	paper
142	off	192	going	242	hard
143	went	193	want	243	near
144	old	194	school	244	sentence
145	number	195	important	245	better
146	great	196	until	246	best
147	tell	197	form	247	across
148	men	198	food	248	during
149	say	199	keep	249	today

(From the 1200 high-frequency writing word list, **SPELLING SOURCEBOOK 1.**)

250	however	300	plants	350	English
251	sure	301	living	351	rest
252	knew	302	black	352	perhaps
253	it's	303	eat	353	certain
254	try	304	short	354	six
255	told	305	United States	355	feel
256	young	306	run	356	fire
257	sun	307	book	357	ready
258	thing	308	gave	358	green
259	whole	309	order	359	yes
260	hear	310	open	360	built
261	example	311	ground	361	special
262	heard	312	cold	362	ran
263	several	313	really	363	full
264	change	314	table	364	town
265	answer	315	remember	365	complete
266	room	316	tree	366	oh
267	sea	317	course	367	person
268	against	318	front	368	hot
269	top	319	American	369	anything
270	turned	320	space	370	hold
271	learn	321	inside	371	state
272	point	322	ago	372	list
273	city	323	sad	373	stood
274	play	324	early	374	hundred
275	toward	325	I'll	375	ten
276	five	326	learned	376	fast
277	himself	327	brought	377	felt
278	usually	328	close	378	kept
279	money	329	nothing	379	notice
280	seen	330	though	380	can't
281	didn't	331	idea	381	strong
282	car	332	before	382	voice
283	morning	333	lived	383	probably
284	I'm	334	became	384	area
285	body	335	add	385	horse
286	upon	336	become	386	matter
287	family	337	grow	387	stand
288	later	338	draw	388	box
289	turn	339	yet	389	start
290	move	340	less	390	that's
291	face	341	wind	391	class
292	door	342	behind	392	piece
293	cut	343	cannot	393	surface
294	done	344	letter	394	river
295	group	345	among	395	common
296	true	346	able	396	stop
297	half	347	dog	397	am
298	red	348	shown	398	talk
299	fish	349	mean	399	whether

400	fine		450	although
401	round		451	sat
402	dark		452	possible
403	past		453	heart
404	ball		454	real
405	girl		455	simple
406	road		456	snow
407	blue		457	rain
408	instead		458	suddenly
409	either		459	easy
410	held		460	leaves
411	already		461	lay
412	warm		462	size
413	gone		463	wild
414	finally		464	weather
415	summer		465	miss
416	understand		466	pattern
417	moon		467	sky
418	animals		468	walked
419	mind		469	main
420	outside		470	someone
421	power		471	center
422	problem		472	field
423	longer		473	stay
424	winter		474	itself
425	deep		475	boat
426	heavy		476	question
427	carefully		477	wide
428	follow		478	least
429	beautiful		479	tiny
430	everyone		480	hour
431	leave		481	happened
432	everything		482	foot
433	game		483	care
434	system		484	low
435	bring		485	else
436	watch		486	gold
437	shall		487	build
438	dry		488	glass
439	within		489	rock
440	floor		490	tall
441	ice		491	alone
442	ship		492	bottom
443	themselves		493	check
444	begin		494	reading
445	fact		495	fall
446	third		496	poor
447	quite		497	map
448	carry		498	friend
449	distance		499	language
			500	job

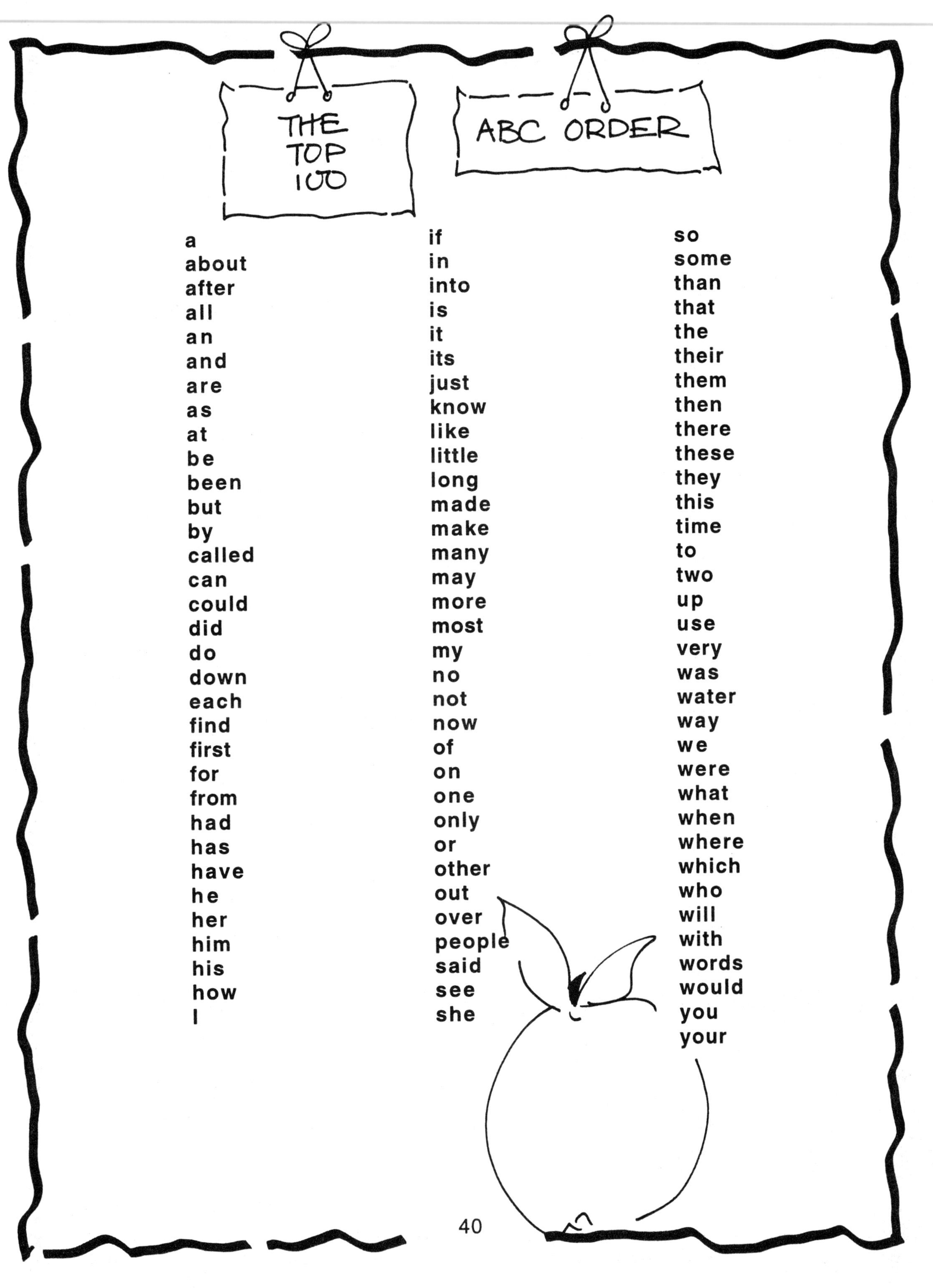

THE TOP 100

ABC ORDER

a
about
after
all
an
and
are
as
at
be
been
but
by
called
can
could
did
do
down
each
find
first
for
from
had
has
have
he
her
him
his
how
I

if
in
into
is
it
its
just
know
like
little
long
made
make
many
may
more
most
my
no
not
now
of
on
one
only
or
other
out
over
people
said
see
she

so
some
than
that
the
their
them
then
there
these
they
this
time
to
two
up
use
very
was
water
way
we
were
what
when
where
which
who
will
with
words
would
you
your

<u>The Core Words</u> constitute the core of the spelling curriculum, its innermost beginning. The Core Words are not the program, but provide the **process** through which the program develops. They are the <u>seed words</u>, likened to the seeds within the core of an apple. The Core Words, or seed words, provide the seeds for creating your spelling programs' strategies, skills, and language-related concepts.

The Core Words can be divided consecutively into <u>grade levels</u> so that all teachers have a set of Core Words from which to begin growing their program. The growth is initiated through the introduction of the Core Words through a Preview, a visual skill-building activity in which the students learn strategies for spelling and proofreading **any word**. This was demonstrated on page 5 and is outlined on page 6. Then, the Core Words serve as seeds for teaching **any** and **all** of the spelling and related language skills and concepts for the purpose of developing long-range spelling and language strategies.

So, the Core Words at any grade level provide the vehicle through which spelling instruction begins. The instructional strategies, the skills, and the concepts recycle themselves through the Core Words multiple times within each grade level and from grade to grade, creating an increasingly sophisticated knowledge of English spelling over time. With the consecutive instructional progression through the Core Words, spelling power grows...and grows...and grows.

Moreover, the Core Words are <u>high-use writing words</u>. The introduction of the Core Words through the Preview initiates an ongoing awareness of their spellings and use. These high-use writing Core Words <u>never change</u> once they are assigned to a grade level. They are the stable centerpiece for spelling instruction.

 CORE WORDS...In your own words__________________________

____

____

____

<u>The Springboard Words and Activities</u> evolve from the Core Words and create learning opportunities that are essential to a complete spelling curriculum. For examples, see page 18 and the pages of explanation that follow.

The activities provide extension through the ongoing opportunities to develop <u>skills and concepts</u> that facilitate strategic understandings. As the skills and concepts are introduced, <u>more words</u> are naturally generated. These are Springboard Words. They not only offer additional word experiences, but also provide word examples for discussion so that students can make generalizations about their language and its correct use. The activities <u>involve students</u> in thoroughly <u>integrated language experiences</u> that can <u>challenge</u> even the most capable spellers. Within the activities, <u>review</u> is built in—specific Core Words, such as the homophones, are recycled within the exercises over and over again. Further, the skills and concepts are recycled to ensure skill mastery.

MORE . . .

There are ready-made Springboard Activities for every Core Word 1-1200 in SOURCEBOOKS 2, 3, and 4 (see <u>Rebecca Sitton's Materials</u> section). Teachers are empowered to choose the activities they want to do and skip the others. Teachers make the activity choices based upon their teaching style, the needs of their students, their time frame, and the curriculum guidelines of their school or school district. Indeed, the Springboard Activities offer teachers curriculum <u>flexibility</u>.

 SPRINGBOARD WORDS and ACTIVITIES...In your own words____________

____

____

____

<u>The Priority Words</u> are the <u>"no excuses" words</u> students are responsible for spelling correctly in their independent, **everyday writing** (as opposed to **process writing** in which 100% accuracy is required). These words must be spelled and proofread with <u>accuracy every day, all day long, for every teacher, in every subject</u>. These words provide the spelling curriculum with student accountability for spelling in writing and ensure the transfer of critical words to writing.

The Priority Words are the <u>highest-frequency writing words</u> that naturally bring the look of literacy to student writing most expediently. The words are listed for the students in alphabetical order, creating an easy-to-use spelling reference. For the homophones on the list, context sentences can be made available. Both the correct spelling and the correct use of the Priority Words are required in the students' writing. If needed, students may check the spellings and use of the Priority Words against their references.

The Priority Words must constitute the <u>major assessment</u> for spelling. It is an authentic assessment because real-world spelling assessment is always made through writing—in business and personal letters, on job applications, and on resumes. Why is authentic assessment through spelling the Priority Words correctly in writing so critical? Because the goal of all spelling instruction is to develop the ability to spell well in writing. The assessment, therefore, must take place within the format for which goal mastery has been set or within the context of writing.

In contrast, traditional spelling tests are usually word list tests or vocabulary-controlled sentence dictation assessments. These are exercises that can contribute to spelling mastery, but a student's performance on either of these cannot determine spelling mastery. <u>Mastery is in writing</u>. And indeed it would contribute negatively toward reaching the goal of spelling mastery to grade students on their mastery of words at some step prior to the goal having been reached. If teachers want to see carryover of words to writing, then the assessment must be from writing. And the high-use words that are assessed are the Priority Words.

PRIORITY WORDS...In your own words________________________________

____

____

____

⬤ CORE (C)... PRIORITY (P)... OR SPRINGBOARD (S)

1. _______ These words are all high-frequency writing words.

2. _______ These alphabetized words may be used as a reference during writing.

3. _______ Words that are generated through language-integrated experiences.

4. _______ The Preview introduces these words to the students for the purpose of practicing the strategies for learning to spell and proofread any word.

5. _______ These words may be likened to seeds that provide the vehicle for growth.

6. _______ The most capable students often generate these words through activities that stimulate additional learning.

7. _______ No excuse is acceptable for misspelling or misusing these words.

8. _______ These words are assigned to grade levels and never change.

9. _______ The mastery of these words is checked through authentic assessment.

10. _______ Words that are used as exemplars for reinforcing skills and concepts.

11. _______ In order of frequency of use is the most expedient way to handle these words.

12. _______ By assessing with these words in everyday writing, students can clearly identify the goal of spelling instruction.

The <u>self-corrected test procedure</u> contributes to developing the visual modality and promoting spelling success.

<u>Visual skills</u> can be taught and learned.

It is easier to develop a visual image of a word if the word is studied in <u>printing</u>.

Students should learn to use an <u>independent word-study procedure</u>.

Spelling should focus on the mastery of <u>high-use writing words</u> that are used in everyday writing.

A basic spelling vocabulary should be expanded to <u>hundreds of additional words</u> for exposure and discussion so that students can make generalizations about their language and its correct use.

Spelling reference lists should be presented in <u>list form</u>, as <u>whole words</u>, in <u>printed writing</u> and in <u>alphabetical</u> order.

There should be <u>no premarking of hard spots</u> on spelling word lists.

Spelling <u>rules should be limited</u> to those that have few exceptions.

Multiple <u>opportunities to write</u> the spelling words in varied ways over time, within the context of writing, contributes to long-term transfer of the words to everyday writing.

It is <u>ineffective to copy words</u> multiple times for practice.

It is <u>ineffective to write words in the air</u>.

<u>Relating spelling to all language skills</u> is essential and appropriate for the spelling curriculum.

All practice should involve <u>writing the words</u>, not orally spelling them.

<u>Authentic spelling assessment</u> must be within students' everyday writing.

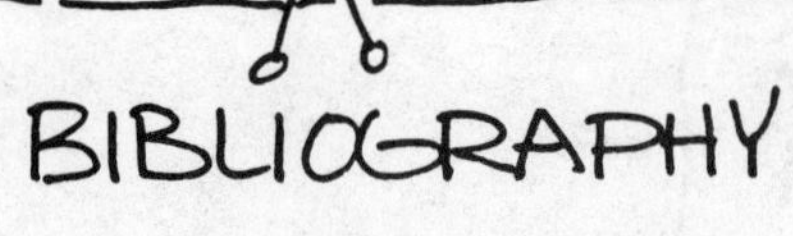

Bartch, Judie. "An Alternative to Spelling: An Integrated Approach." *Language Arts*, Vol. 69, No. 6, 1992.

Bodycott, Peter. "Personalizing Spelling Instruction." *Childhood Education*, Vol. 69, No. 4, 1993.

Carroll, J. B., Peter Davies, and Barry Richman. *The American Heritage Word Frequency Book.* New York: Houghton Mifflin, 1971.

Dale, Edgar, and Joseph O'Rourke. *The Living Word Vocabulary*. Chicago: World Book-Childcraft International, Inc., 1981.

DiStefano, Philip, and Patricia Hagerty. "Teaching Spelling at the Elementary Level," *The Reading Teacher*, Vol, 38, January, 1985.

Fitzsimmons, Robert J., and Bradley M. Loomer. *Spelling: The Research Basis.* Iowa City: The University of Iowa, 1980.

Gentry, J. Richard, and Edmund H. Henderson. "Three Steps to Teaching Beginning Readers to Spell." *The Reading Teacher*, Vol. 31, March, 1978.

Graham, Steve. "Evaluating Spelling Programs and Materials." *Teaching Exceptional Children.* Vol. 17, No. 4, Summer, 1985.

Greene, Henry A., and Bradley M. Loomer. *The New Iowa Spelling Scale.* Iowa City: The University of Iowa, 1977.

Haber, Ralph Norman, and Lyn R. Haber. "The Shape of a Word Can Specify Its Meaning." *Reading Research Quarterly*, Vol. XVI, No. 3. Newark, DE: International Reading Association, Inc., 1981.

Hagerty, Patricia. "Comparative Analysis of High Frequency Words Found in Commercial Spelling Series and Misspelled in Students' Writing to a Standard Measure of Word Frequency." Ed.D. Thesis, University of Colorado, 1981.

Hanna, Paul R., Richard E. Hodges, and Jean S. Hanna. *Spelling: Structure and Strategies.* Boston: Houghton Mifflin, 1971.

Harp, Bill. "When the Principal Asks, 'Why Are Your Kids Giving Each Other Spelling Tests?'" *Reading Teacher*, Vol. 41, No. 7, March, 1988.

Henderson, Edmund H. *Teaching Spelling.* Boston: Houghton Mifflin, 1985.

Henderson, Edmund H., and Shane Templeton. "A Developmental Perspective of Formal Spelling Instruction Through Alphabet, Pattern, and Meaning." *Elementary School Journal*, Vol. 66, No. 3, 1986.

Hillerich, Robert L. "Spelling: To Teach Not Just to Observe." *Illinois Schools Journal*, Vol. 66, No. 2, 1987.

Horn, Ernest. *A Basic Writing Vocabulary: 10,000 Frequently Used Words in Writing.* Monograph First Series, No. 4. Iowa City: The University of Iowa, 1926.

Horn, Thomas. "The Effect of the Corrected Test on Learning to Spell." Master's Thesis, The University of Iowa, 1946.

Jongsma, K. "Reading-Spelling Links." *The Reading Teacher*, Vol. 43, No. 8, 1990.

MORE . . .

...MORE...BIBLIOGRAPHY REFERENCES...

Kingsley, J. H. "The Test-Study Method Versus Study-Test Method in Spelling." *Elementary School Journal*, Vol. 24. Chicago: The University of Chicago Press, 1923.

Learning Magazine, "What Works In Spelling," September, 1995.

Lutz, Elaine. "ERIC/RCS Report: Invented Spelling and Spelling Development." *Language Arts*, Vol. 63, No. 7, November, 1986.

Morris, Darrell. "Meeting the Needs of Poor Spellers in the Elementary School: A Developmental Prospective." *Illinois Schools Journal*, Vol. 66, No. 2, 1987.

Novelli, Joan. "Strategies for Spelling Success." *Instructor*, Vol. 102, No. 9, 1993.

O'Flahavan, John F., and Renee Blassberg. "Toward an Embedded Model of Spelling Instruction for Emergent Literates." *Language Arts*, Vol. 69, No. 6, 1992.

Read, Charles, and Richard Hodges. "Spelling." *Encyclopedia of Educational Research*, 5th edition, New York: Macmillan, 1982.

Routman, Regie. "The Uses and Abuses of Invented Spelling." *Instructor*, Vol. 102, No. 9, 1993.

Schlagal, Robert C., and Joy Harris Schlagal. "The Integral Character of Spelling: Teaching Strategies for Multiple Purposes." *Language Arts*, Vol. 69, No. 6, 1992.

Sensenbaugh, Roger. "Spelling and the Language Arts." *Language Arts*, Vol. 69, No. 6, 1992.

Sitton, Rebecca A. "Spelling Instruction: A Dilemma for the Resource Specialist." *California Resource Specialists Journal*, Vol. 10, No. 5, 1990.

Sitton, Rebecca A. "Spelling: Three Critical Questions to Consider." *Conversations*, Curriculum Associates, No. 2, Spring, 1991.

Sitton, Rebecca A. "A Turning Point: Three Critical Connections in the Spelling Curriculum for the Nineties." *The California Reader*, Vol. 23, No. 4, 1990.

Sowers, Susan. "Six Questions Teachers Ask About Invented Spellings." *Understanding Writing: Ways of Observing, Learning & Thinking*. Eds. Thomas Newkirk and Nancie Atwell. Portsmouth, NH: Heinemann, 1986. 47-56.

Stetson, Elton, Wendy Taylor, and Frances J. Boutin. *Eighty Years of Theory and Practice in Spelling: Those Who Wrote the Programs Forgot to Read the Literature*. Clearwater, FL: National Reading Conference, 1982.

Templeton, Shane. "New Trends in an Historical Perspective: Old Story, New Resolution--Sound and Meaning in Spelling." *Language Arts*, Vol. 69, No. 6, 1992.

Templeton, Shane. "Synthesis of Research on the Learning and Teaching of Spelling." *Educational Leadership*, Vol. 43, March, 1986.

Thorndike, Edward L., and Irving Lorge. *The Teacher's Word Book of 30,000 Words*. New York: Columbia University, 1944.

Wilde, Sandra. "A Proposal for a New Spelling Curriculum." *Elementary School Journal*, Vol. 90, No. 3, 1990.

Article 1

REPRINT: Rebecca Sitton's SPELLING SOURCEBOOK 1
Northwest Textbook, Portland, OR
503-639-3193

Defining the Spelling Curriculum

Why is spelling important?

Spelling is a skill. It is a basic communication skill. And it *is* important. Regardless of how well writers express their ideas in writing, if their writing in its final form has misspellings, the worth of the message is diminished in the eyes of the reader. In fact, the personal worth of the writer may also be diminished.

Ask employers if misspellings on job applications and resumes influence their opinion of applicants. Ask yourself how your own opinion of a person you've never met might be affected if his or her letter to you contains misspellings. Spelling errors convey a subtle message of limited knowledge or a lack of conscientious effort on the part of the writer.

Acceptance, then, is one reason for teaching spelling. Writing that conforms to conventional English orthography is more acceptable to the reader. But there is another reason for teaching spelling. Writers who have a mental bank of words that they can spell correctly with ease while writing have a fluidity to their writing that poor spellers do not have.

All teachers have observed students who "turn off" to writing because they lack a mental bank of spelling words from which to draw as they write. These students learn that the less they write, the less they misspell. They lack a ready resource for spelling the words they need as they write. Spelling instruction helps students develop a mental bank of high-use words. Then, as they write, they can focus their attention on the content of the message being written, rather than on the mechanics of writing it.

Why will technology never make spelling instruction obsolete?

Yet, these reasons do not convince some people that spelling is an essential skill. They point out that dictionaries are affordable and easily available. Further, technology is capable of providing spelling aid through spell-checkers and grammar-checkers on word processors. Shouldn't writers be taught to use these spelling resources? Yes—but they're not enough.

The teaching of computation was not forsaken when calculators became a household item. However, neither a calculator nor a spell-checker can think . . . and there is no substitute for thinking. A spell-checker does not alert the writer to an incorrectly spelled word when the spelling would be correct for another word. For instance, the errors in this sentence do not register on a spell-checker, nor do all the errors register on a grammar-checker:

Their our for pairs. (There are four pears.)

Advocates for abandoning the spelling curriculum go on to cite research that clearly indicates that spelling is developmental. They say that if educators would familiarize themselves with the natural, predictable steps through which children progress as they acquire spelling skills, a spelling program would no longer make good sense.

How do developmental skills develop?

Yes, spelling is developmental. Much research reports the developmental nature of spelling. These reports are highly interesting and factual reading. But isn't the acquisition of all skills developmental? Why single out spelling as being unique? Children learn to count before they are taught to add . . . they learn to add before they are taught to multiply—learning number concepts is developmental. And does it logically follow that if something is developmental, it cannot or should not be taught? Do all developmental skills develop completely naturally, making a curriculum for their mastery unnecessary?

47

Why is a curriculum necessary?

The first obligation of conscientious educators is to be knowledgeable of how students develop and learn. Then, however, they must apply this knowledge to implement instructional strategies to enhance student learning. A stated curriculum provides the foundation for this instruction and suggests strategies for achieving, or developing, the desired learning. And it is irresponsible to assume that all teachers can intuitively create such a curriculum while juggling the demands of everyday instruction.

So, yes, the *Spelling Sourcebooks do* call for a stated spelling curriculum, albeit a significant departure from traditional spelling methodology. Indeed, the scope and sequence of the *Spelling Sourcebook* curriculum is sensitive to the developmental steps of spelling acquisition, but provides teachers with options for contributing to spelling growth as their students develop as writers. Just knowing the developmental stages of spelling growth does not provide teachers with a plan for what to do Monday with a classroom full of students.

What is traditional about the Sourcebook curriculum? What is nontraditional?

The *Spelling Sourcebook* curriculum is the spelling complement to a literature-based, writing-rich classroom steeped in language experiences. Traditional, commonsense spelling skills and their application in writing are built into the methodology, but this is done in nontraditional ways. Teachers are empowered through the *Spelling Sourcebooks* to make many curriculum decisions that the traditional spelling books once made for them. These decisions that customize spelling instruction to accommodate a variety of needs are made from a menu of carefully researched options, all of which are bonded to writing and research.

Therefore, the *Spelling Sourcebook* curriculum is considerably more flexible, less structured than that of the traditional spelling series. It may be that some teachers will initially feel uncomfortable with the freedom this flexibility provides. Nonetheless, sufficient structure is provided so that spelling instruction is *not* incidental. Spelling instruction using the *Spelling Sourcebook* methodology, follows a clear and logical plan.

How do current spelling instructional outcomes measure up to employers' expectations for workplace literacy?

Basic literacy, specifically spelling competence, must be one of education's ensured outcomes. Employers are not asking too much of educators when they plead for graduates to be equipped with basic language know-how skills to function literately in the workplace. Spelling high-use words consistently correctly is a component of this literacy.

Unfortunately, facts clearly indicate that many students are not currently learning to spell these high-use words correctly in their everyday writing. A look at their writing verifies this. Often even the most capable students misspell commonly-used words in their writing.

Why is the Friday Test an invalid assessment?

Yes, these students spell the words correctly on a spelling test! But spelling on a spelling test is not an authentic assessment of spelling facility. Employers do not give spelling tests on Friday to determine whether their employees are literate written communicators. Nonetheless, some teachers may believe they have successfully taught spelling when their students score well on a dictated list of words written correctly on demand in isolation, apart from writing. This test is the traditional weekly "Friday Spelling Test."

Ironically, the words on these tests are often the difficult, seldom-used words. Spelling instruction, then, frequently encourages memorizing letter sequences of words that have little pertinence for everyday writing . . . week after week for the Friday Test.

Traditionally, the grades on these tests, rather than the presence or absence of misspelled words in the students' writing, become the measure of students' spelling ability. It is not unusual for students to receive top spelling grades, yet show a serious lack of attention to spelling in their writing. What message does this give the student writer?

Why aren't students transferring spelling skills into writing?

Are students incapable of learning to spell words correctly in their everyday writing? No, of course students can learn to spell in their writing! Then why haven't they learned? The answer is an obvious one. Students are not spelling words responsibly in their everyday writing because they don't have to.

Most educators simply don't expect students to spell correctly in their everyday writing. "Oh, I *do* expect my students to spell!" object some teachers. They adamantly believe that they maintain high standards for spelling in writing because they firmly tell their students to proofread their papers. Yet, students know that their spelling grades are based on spelling words correctly on a test, not on spelling in everyday assignments across the curriculum. Again, what message does this give the student writer? Or . . . what message does it give the student writer if *no* grades are given for spelling?

In fact, be forewarned . . . inattention to spelling literacy jeopardizes the language-centered approach to learning, as well as the credibility of teachers and schools. Students must be expected to spell an increasing number of high-use words correctly in their writing as they mature as writers. This does not inhibit their creativity. It is basic literacy. In fact, if students learn that it's acceptable to spell irresponsibly throughout their schooling, serious problems may develop when they later find that employers have higher expectations for them than their teachers had. Worst case, their job applications are not considered because of inexcusable spelling errors.

How does a traditional definition of spelling mastery differ from the new one?

Spelling is not how many words a teacher "covers," nor how many words a student spells correctly on a spelling test, albeit a Friday Test or a standardized spelling test. Covering words and then testing students on them reflect an inaccurate concept of spelling mastery. Spelling mastery is the ability to spell words correctly in everyday writing.

Can schools accommodate this definition of spelling mastery? Yes, but "spelling for writing" will not evolve through traditional spelling instructional methods and assessment tools. The old-time spelling textbooks and the philosophy on which they were founded must *go*.

"No spelling book? Then what will teachers do for spelling?" The spelling book is . . . well, traditional. Yet, most educators concede that the traditional spelling program has failed. If spelling mastery means spelling well in everyday writing, then the spelling textbooks have not satisfactorily met the challenge. Nonetheless, the books are difficult to do without . . . they have conveniently filled a time frame that provides seatwork practice within a subject area that teachers are expected to teach . . . and that parents expect their children to learn.

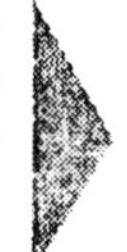

What role has the traditional spelling textbook served?

Contrary to time-honored tradition, spelling can successfully be taught without the aid of the customary student spelling textbooks. In fact, in some instances these spelling textbooks may have hindered the acquisition of spelling skills in writing. Why? Because the spelling books became the spelling curriculum. There were 36 weekly units of words, and conscientious teachers felt an admirable obligation to teach and test every one of them. And *that* was spelling.

Instruction in the spelling books did not consider the needs of the student writers. It did not encourage students to spell and proofread outside of the spelling book. Spelling became an isolated subject, apart from purposeful writing, void of pertinence and utility.

However, there is no guarantee that removing the spelling textbooks from classrooms will result in better spelling instruction. Teachers in classrooms without spelling textbooks have clearly shown this to be true. Unless the old spelling programs are replaced with practical, more effective ways of teaching spelling that produce visible spelling proficiencies in writing, the problem remains unsolved. The solution requires that spelling find a meaningful role within the integrated curriculum. This necessitates a change in conventional thinking about what spelling mastery is and when it has been achieved. This change may not be easy, but it will be exciting and the results will be gratifying . . . and the change is overdue.

What alternative is there to "textbook" spelling?

The *Spelling Sourcebook* Series provides the guidelines for this change. The methodology, as suggested through the *Spelling Sourcebooks*, is a departure from the "tired and traditional" spelling textbook programs. The *Spelling Sourcebook* Series shows forward-looking educators how to develop and use a spelling program of their own . . . one *without* student textbooks. It focuses on research-based methods to teach high-frequency writing words within writing-rich classrooms across the curriculum. It flexibly meets the needs and interests of developing writers as they write. It outlines strategies for authentically assessing spelling. The *Spelling Sourcebook* Series shows educators how to make spelling a meaningful part of the language-integrated, literature-based curriculum with results where spelling really counts . . . in everyday writing.

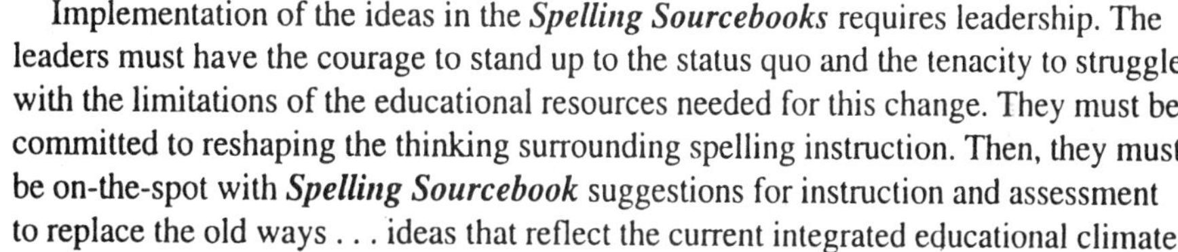

How will changes in the spelling curriculum emerge?

Implementation of the ideas in the *Spelling Sourcebooks* requires leadership. The leaders must have the courage to stand up to the status quo and the tenacity to struggle with the limitations of the educational resources needed for this change. They must be committed to reshaping the thinking surrounding spelling instruction. Then, they must be on-the-spot with *Spelling Sourcebook* suggestions for instruction and assessment to replace the old ways . . . ideas that reflect the current integrated educational climate.

This new leadership role is not for everyone. It is certainly not for those educators incapable of seeing the future; it is not for those who have a hundred reasons why students can't or shouldn't be expected to spell; it is not for those who avoid the issue by promising that spelling skills will develop naturally . . . *later;* it is not for the nay sayers and complainers undaunted by cries for school reform. It is, however, for those who have a passion for educational excellence and a sense of purpose dedicated to equipping all students with language literacy. Educators open to this challenge, read on.

As children learn to speak, approximations are accepted and encouraged. Later when children gain language proficiency, corrections are made. Invented spellings parallel the approximations that children make while learning to talk. Likewise, as children begin to write, approximations are natural. But later, invented spellings need to be phased out and replaced with conventional spelling.

This spelling transition must begin early for the highest-use words, usually by the second half of grade one. Students in grade one write often. If the highest-use words (the, of, and, a, to, in, is, you) are written incorrectly repeatedly, the misspellings are reinforced and become increasingly difficult to change.

Teachers can begin the transition to conventional spellings in a positive, motivational way. They can explain the "system" authors use to make their stories easy to read...the system of spelling words just one way. Teachers can begin by asking students to proofread for "the" in their stories. Then they can add "of" and "and" after students demonstrate proficiency with "the." Through many positive writing opportunities, the transition to conventional spellings for these high-use words takes place effortlessly and helps students develop a conscientious attitude toward spelling.

It once was thought that invented spellings would not lead to the formation of bad spelling habits. However, the evidence began mounting that led educators to modify this belief. The totality of the invented-spelling philosophy reduced the importance of spelling in the minds of both teachers and students. The outcome emerged as major student spelling deficiencies in writing. But, initial acceptance of invented spellings cannot be blamed for this. The culprit, as I see it, is the philosophy that any attention to spelling in writing is "inappropriate" and that spelling skills will "naturally" develop...later.

Instead, teachers need a plan for the development of spelling skills in writing. They need confirmation that spelling literacy is indeed an instructional goal. It defies common sense to believe that all students will develop spelling skills if there is no curriculum to foster an attention to spelling. A comfortable, but certain, transition must be made to conventional spellings or the look of literacy will be forever lacking in students' writing.

FAVORITE FOLKLORE AND FAIRY TALES ARE EXAMPLES OF OUR CULTURAL HERITAGE AND ARE OFTEN A PART OF THE SCHOOL CURRICULUM AT ALL LEVELS OF INSTRUCTION.

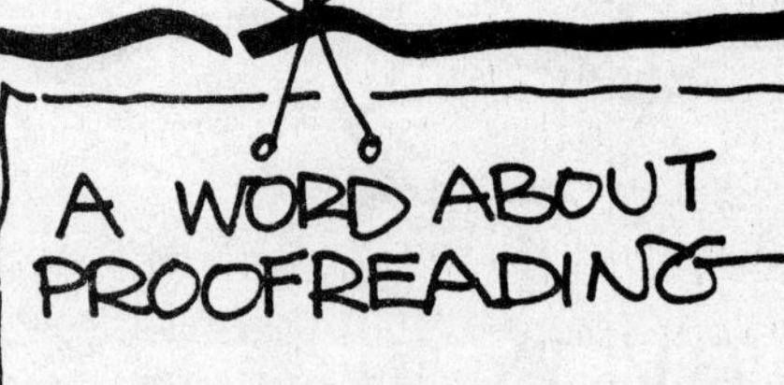

The acquisition of spelling and proofreading skills go hand in hand. Indeed, if a student spells well on tests but cannot proofread known words in daily writing, the student cannot spell. So knowing how to proofread is an important part of spelling well.

Proofreading acquisition has two learning phases. The first is learning <u>how to</u> proofread. The second is <u>application</u> of proofreading skills in writing. Learning <u>how to</u> proofread is dependent upon the development of visual skills—learning how to look at each letter of a word in sequence. This skill can, in part, be developed through consistent and careful use of the self-corrected test procedure and a word-study procedure. Practice exercises that emphasize visual skills are also essential. Proofreading <u>application</u> occurs in the context of a student's writing. But, it does little good to expect students to effectively proofread if they have not been taught the prerequisite "how to" skills.

Teachers often complain that students do not "see" their misspellings in writing. Even when students say they have proofread their work, they often read what they think they wrote, rather than what is really there. The meaning, not the mechanics, is taking precedence.

This is exactly what we should expect our students to do considering the focus of our reading instruction every day, year after year. As students learn to read, they quickly replace sound-it-out and whole-word reading with sophisticated "reading for meaning" strategies. Teachers teach students to read for meaning by digesting phrases of information at a glance. This is emphasized in all reading instruction and reinforced in the content areas as students read to learn.

In other words, students are taught in reading <u>not</u> to look at the exact letter sequences of words. They would never become fluent readers if they did! Yet, to be an effective speller and proofreader, students must learn to refocus on the minute details of words.

One function of spelling and proofreading instruction and practice is to provide students with opportunities to learn to "see" words differently for spelling and proofreading than they do for reading. Without this visual training, followed by abundant opportunities for application, proofreading will continue to suffer within the writing process...and make it appear as though little spelling has been taught.

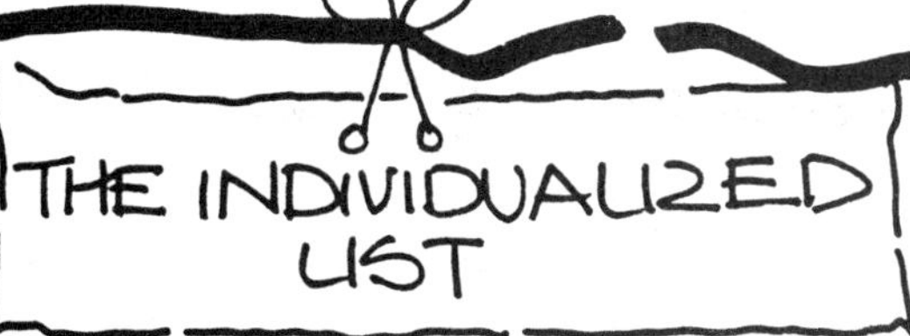

An Individualized List of spelling words for each student can round out your spelling program to complement your basic instruction.

What is the Individualized List?

This list accommodates an individual student's words. Each student has one.

What words might students record on an Individualized List?

1. Priority Words students misspelled or misused on the papers selected at random from everyday writing pieces. Before the students hand their corrected papers back, they can add the misspelled or misused Priority Words to their Individualized List.

2. Priority Words misspelled or misused on a dictation activity. Once these words are identified, students can add them to their Individualized List.

3. Core Words missed on the Core Word Review. Though all students should get 100% on their Review, if they do not, then the words missed can go onto their Individualized List.

4. Words personally important to your students. Students can learn to spell the name of their city, state, school, teacher, principal, street on which they live, the names of their friends and relatives, etc., by adding them to their Individualized List.

5. Words individual students want to learn—*bear, dinosaur, awesome*. Over time, students can be taught to choose words that have writing relevance. The more capable student writers would likely use this option more, as they would need more specialized words for their writing pieces.

6. Words the teacher feels a student would benefit from knowing how to spell, such as words generated from Springboard Activities. If *help* is a Core Word and the Springboard Activity for *help* asks students to generate its other word forms and use them in context, then perhaps *helpless* and *helpful* could be added to the Individualized List for capable students.

7. Words with writing relevance that a parent wants their child to learn. These words might include the city and state in which the grandparents live so that the student can address an envelope correctly when a letter is sent from home, the occupations of the parents, or words often included on the family grocery list.

MORE...

1. Students can record the words in an alphabetized booklet using the blackline master titled Words to Learn. See the reproducible master section of this handbook for this master and directions for its use.

2. Students might record the words in a booklet with sheets of regular writing paper stapled together with a construction paper cover.

3. Some teachers ask their students to record these words in their QUICK-WORD HANDBOOKS. (See Rebecca Sitton's Materials section of this handbook.)

4. A teacher-made blackline master titled "My Individualized List" can serve to collect these words.

5. A single sheet of writing paper can be used to list these words. Students can keep this sheet of paper in a special writing folder.

6. A 5"x7" index card can be used for these words. Students each have an index card with their name on it. The card is given to the student each time a paper with Priority Word errors is returned to the student for correction. The Priority Words misspelled or misused on the paper are corrected, then recorded on the index card. Next, the paper and the card are returned to the teacher. When students are asked to record other words on their Individualized List, their card can be returned to them for the recording.

7. Younger students may like to keep their words on small word cards in which a hole is punched. The words can be kept together with a shower curtain ring, key ring, or notebook ring.

Should the words on the Individualized List be studied, tested, and graded?

Approximately every two to three weeks, students should study the words that have been accumulating on their Individualized List. The lists should be checked to be sure that the words have been recorded on the lists with accurate spellings. Then the students can study the words at school or at home. At school they could study their words independently or in pairs. The best method for study is the independent word-study procedure (see page 3).

Then students can be tested on their words. Students can be paired for partner testing. Partners can test each other using the self-corrected test procedure (see page 6). This procedure should be familiar to the students and they should administer it to each other exactly the way the teacher administers it to the class during the Word Preview.

During this paired testing, the teacher can circulate through the classroom monitoring the activity and providing occasional assistance, especially with homophone context sentences. As students test each other, if the words are spelled correctly by their partner, a check can go next to the word on their list. If the word is not spelled correctly, no check mark is made and the word carries over to the next pair testing activity.

A grade for this test? Students often assess the importance of an activity by whether it is graded and/or collected for teacher review. To attach importance to this paired testing activity, students could write their scores on their tests and hand them in to the teacher. However, real spelling mastery is never assessed by testing words in isolation, apart from everyday writing. So, the real grade will be derived from the random samples of students' everyday writing papers, as discussed in the seminar.

Should teacher instruction be provided for words on the Individualized Lists?

Teachers should regularly review the Individualized Lists for diagnostic information critical to conscientious instruction. If the students' lists reveal that a handful of students persistently misuse the homophones *to*, *two*, and *too*, then a mini-lesson for these students would be appropriate. Indeed, these Individualized Lists can provide ongoing information about the spelling errors of specific students. Teachers can use the information to effectively group students for instruction that concisely meets their spelling needs.

Correcting misspellings in student writing must always keep the integrity of the paper (and the writer) intact. However, with students writing as much as they currently are in our writing-rich classrooms, not all papers can be checked for spelling and keep the sanity of the teacher intact.

For writing-as-a-process papers, the first draft has no spelling expectations; the final copy must have all words spelled correctly. For everyday writing papers (all writing with the exception of writing-as-a-process papers), the expectation is to spell the Priority Words, correctly...as well as any topical reference words provided.

Everyday writing papers can be selected at random, unannounced for correcting. Some papers can be chosen from students on Monday, some Tuesday, and so on. Students should feel that every time they produce an everyday writing paper in any subject for any teacher, it could be chosen for a spelling evaluation. Indeed, it's therefore important for teachers to be unpredictable when selections are made.

Teachers can develop a system for checking the spelling of Priority Words or they can choose a method among these:

1. Write at the bottom of the paper the Priority Word errors.
2. Place a dot in the margin to indicate on which writing line a mistake occurred.
3. Place a numeral on the paper to indicate the number of Priority Word errors that were made. (If this is initially too difficult, introduce the method by asking students to find their errors cooperatively with a partner.)
4. Attach a sticky-note to the paper on which is written the Priority Word errors.
5. Underline or circle the Priority Word errors.
6. Use a highlighter pen to discreetly signal Priority Word errors.

It is unnecessary to mark the errors on an entire paper selected for assessment. Most teachers prefer to select 2-3 paragraphs or a set number of lines from each writing piece they choose for assessment. This is an effective solution to the time constraints all teachers face with paper correction. It allows teachers to review more students' papers more often. And the more often papers can be selected for feedback regarding how well students are meeting the spelling expectation, the more seriously the expectation is perceived. Teachers simply want to convey to students the message that there are every-time-you-write expectations for spelling—that they are randomly, but routinely **looking**...and they **care**.

After the checking, the papers should be returned to the students. The students are responsible for correcting their errors. They do not need to rewrite the entire assignment, just correct the errors indicated. Next the students can return their corrected papers to the teacher or check the corrections with a designated student or teaching assistant.

Standardized spelling tests measure <u>only</u> the ability to take a standardized spelling test. For this reason, forward-thinking educators are rethinking standardized spelling tests. They are questioning the expense, time, and utility of tests that produce invalid results. Fortunately, many educators are now willing to stand up to the status quo and forego standardized spelling tests. However, until these tests are abolished, there are strategies for improving scores.

The key prerequisite for a high standardized spelling score is knowing how to proofread. These tests <u>all use a proofreading format</u>. For example, the Texas TAAS test and the ITBS test a student's ability to proofread. The spelling methodology suggested in the seminar profoundly emphasizes proofreading—its instruction, practice, and everyday application. This intensive proofreading preparatory work provides students with standardized test-taking skills like nothing else has every done. In fact, schools now report <u>increased standardized spelling test scores with the use of Rebecca Sitton's spelling methodology</u>.

Further, the seminar methodology serves students well in another way for taking standardized tests. As students become engaged in the Springboard Activities, they not only have hundreds of additional word experiences, but they learn to make reasonable generalizations about English spellings. For example, a Springboard Activity with the Core Word "point" challenges students to find and write dozens of words that contain an *oi* or *oy* vowel pattern. Students learn that the *oi* is considerably (70%) more prominent in English for spelling the sound that these two vowels make. However, if the sound is at the end of a word, it is always spelled with *oy*. Activities like this one teach students <u>spelling strategies that they can apply during spelling standardized</u> <u>test taking</u>, as well as throughout their life.

Scores can also be raised by practicing the test format. Test-like blacklines can be administered to students that use the same directions, format, and time frame of the tests—but not the same words. This creates test-wise students.

But is there a valid substitute for standardized spelling tests? <u>The only valid test of spelling is within writing</u>. Progress is being made by astute educators to evaluate spelling within writing samples. Four to six times a year, students are given a topic on which to write without the aid of spelling references. Then the spellings for high-use words within a predetermined bank, such as the top 100 words, are checked. This information can become a part of students' portfolios, and/or it can be used to make student comparisons for growth over time. These comparisons may include performance among grade-level classes and/or comparisons among different grades within a school or district.

Spelling in writing CAN be achieved and this ability CAN be measured. The way in which spelling ability is measured often determines the focus for instruction. Even if standardized spelling tests must still be administered, spelling in writing should be evaluated. This emphasis alone can have dramatic results for creating students who can spell where it really counts—in their everyday writing.

Report Card grading is "a communication of progress toward meeting expectations," such as through a letter grade (A-F), a number (1-5), a mark (+, -), a rubric, a written statement, or a face-to-face conversation. Grading systems differ. For any grading system to "work," students must know what is expected, how to day-by-day meet the expectation, and have regular feedback to monitor their own achievement. The trend for reporting spelling grades is to make it a *prominent grade*, enhancing student accountability and parent relations. If the spelling grade on the Report Card is currently insufficient, a supplement could be added (see Spelling Progress Report, next page).

The only authentic evaluation for spelling is students' writing. This, then must be the most important factor for grading spelling. So, which words need to be spelled correctly in writing? If the writing is a part of the writing process, then the final copy must be perfect. Writing that does not progress through multiple stages to an error-free final copy, is everyday writing. For everyday writing, students should nonetheless have some level of spelling accuracy. This can be achieved through the Priority Words (the high-use no-excuse words) and any topical words added to the list.

To grade spelling, teachers should take random samples of everyday writing to determine the level of accuracy for spelling. Two or three paragraphs can be bracketed on papers selected for evaluation (or a few lines for primary writers). This is checked against the current set of Priority Words (see Correcting Spelling Errors). After the students have corrected their errors, these papers can be saved in a file labeled for each student for later reference. Some teachers ask students to note their errors on a personal Record Keeper (see Blackline Record Keepers in SPELLING SOURCEBOOK 1) that can either be attached to the corrected paper or kept as a cumulative record of errors.

Students who have made no Priority errors at the end of the grading period are the only candidates for the top evaluation (high standards for spelling Priority Words are essential!). Other factors that could also be considered are: (1) effort and completion of Springboard Activities, (2) ability to reach an error-free paper during a writing-process piece, (3) ability to maintain spelling accuracy on a no-reference write (no Priority Word references), (4) performance on sentence dictation and cloze activities (available for high-use words in the SPELLING SOURCEBOOK REVIEWS).

If a percentage grade is required, the random writing samples must function as the largest part of the 100% total—no less than 50% of the grade, but could be as high as 80-90% of the grade. The remaining percentage can be divided up among any or all of the above factors. Educators must predetermine this as a group.

Grading can be a constructive element toward motivation and increased achievement if it is handled in a positive way. Students need routine feedback before the final grade is awarded. If they are kept apprised of their progress, they can take the initiative to influence their achievement. Some students need more feedback than others, some need higher expectations than others, some need more monitoring than others. All of these factors influence grading, motivation, and achievement and can be adjusted by the guiding teacher in the classroom.

Name____

SPELLING PROGRESS REPORT

Marking Code:
    3 (exceeds expectations)
    2 (meets expectations)
    1 (falls below expectations)
    X (not graded this quarter)

Grading Quarters:	**1st**	**2nd**	**3rd**	**4th**
Uses correct spelling in everyday writing	____	____	____	____
Completes spelling skill-building activities	____	____	____	____

Comments:____

____

____

____

____

Parent Signature   _______________________________

                                 ____

                                 ____

                                 ____

Teaching word patterns can help students expand their vocabularies and spelling skills. When a word appears in the spelling list that illustrates a structural pattern used in many other words, have students brainstorm for those words.

Remember, do not organize your word lists by patterns. Students learn to spell words more quickly in patterned lists, but they also forget them more quickly!

 Here are examples of many patterns and words that employ them:

cab, crab, drab, gab, grab, jab, scab, slab, stab, tab

brace, face, grace, lace, mace, pace, place, race, space, trace

back, black, clack, crack, hack, Jack, knack, lack, pack, quack, rack, sack, shack, smack, snack, stack, tack, track, whack

bad, clad, dad, fad, glad, had, lad, mad, pad, sad, shad, tad

bade, blade, fade, glade, grade, jade, made, shade, spade, trade, wade

bag, brag, drag, flag, gag, hag, lag, nag, rag, sag, shag, slag, snag, stag, swag, tag, wag

bail, fail, frail, hail, jail, mail, nail, pail, quail, rail, sail, snail, tail, trail, wail

brain, chain, drain, gain, grain, lain, main, pain, plain, rain, slain, Spain, sprain, stain, strain, train, vain

air, chair, fair, flair, hair, lair, pair, stair

bake, brake, cake, drake, fake, flake, Jake, lake, make, quake, rake, sake, shake, snake, stake, take, wake

ball, call, fall, gall, hall, mall, small, squall, stall, tall, wall

clam, cram, dam, ham, jam, ram, sham, slam, tram, yam

blame, came, dame, fame, flame, frame, game, lame, name, same, shame, tame

camp, champ, clamp, cramp, damp, lamp, ramp, scamp, stamp, tramp

MORE . . .

ban, bran, can, clan, Dan, fan, man, pan, plan, ran, scan, span, tan, than, van

band, bland, brand, gland, grand, hand, land, sand, stand, strand

cane, crane, lane, mane, pane, plane, sane, vane

bang, clang, fang, gang, hang, pang, rang, sang, slang, sprang, tang

bank, blank, clank, crank, drank, Frank, plank, prank, rank, sank, shrank, spank, tank, thank, yank

cap, chap, clap, flap, gap, lap, map, nap, rap, sap, scrap, slap, snap, strap, tap, trap, wrap

bar, car, char, far, jar, mar, scar, spar, star, tar

bare, blare, care, dare, fare, flare, glare, mare, rare, scare, share, snare, spare, square, stare

bark, dark, hark, lark, mark, park, shark, spark, stark

bash, brash, cash, clash, crash, dash, flash, gash, hash, lash, mash, rash, sash, slash, smash, stash, thrash, trash

bat, brat, cat, chat, fat, flat, gnat, hat, mat, pat, rat, sat, scat, slat, spat, that, vat

crate, date, fate, gate, grate, hate, late, mate, plate, rate, skate, state

brave, cave, crave, gave, grave, pave, rave, save, shave, slave, wave

claw, draw, flaw, gnaw, jaw, law, paw, raw, saw, squaw, straw

bay, clay, cray, day, fray, gay, gray, hay, jay, lay, may, pay, play, pray, ray, say, slay, spray, stay, stray, tray, way

bread, dead, dread, head, lead, read, spread, thread, tread

beak, bleak, creak, leak, peak, sneak, speak, squeak, streak, teak, weak

deal, heal, meal, peal, real, seal, squeal, steal, veal, zeal

beam, cream, dream, gleam, ream, scream, seam, steam, stream, team

clear, dear, fear, gear, hear, near, rear, sear, shear, smear, spear, tear, year

MORE . . .

beat, bleat, cheat, cleat, feat, heat, meat, neat, peat, pleat, seat, treat, wheat

bed, bled, bred, fed, fled, led, Ned, red, shed, shred, sled, sped, wed

bleed, breed, creed, deed, feed, freed, greed, heed, need, reed, seed, speed, steed, weed

cheek, creek, leek, meek, peek, seek, sleek, week

cheep, creep, deep, jeep, keep, peep, seep, sheep, sleep, steep, sweep, weep

beet, feet, fleet, greet, meet, sheet, sleet, street, sweet, tweet

bell, cell, dell, dwell, fell, jell, quell, sell, shell, smell, spell, swell, tell, well, yell

den, hen, men, pen, ten, then, when, wren, yen

bend, blend, end, fend, lend, mend, send, spend, tend, trend, vend

bent, cent, dent, gent, lent, rent, scent, sent, spent, tent, vent, went

best, chest, crest, guest, jest, lest, nest, pest, quest, rest, test, vest, west, zest

bet, fret, get, jet, let, met, net, pet, set, wet, yet

blew, brew, chew, crew, dew, drew, few, flew, hew, knew, pew, screw, stew, threw

dice, lice, mice, nice, price, rice, slice, spice, splice, twice, vice

brick, chick, click, flick, kick, lick, pick, quick, sick, slick, stick, thick, tick, trick, wick

bid, did, grid, hid, kid, lid, rid, skid, slid, squid

bride, chide, glide, hide, pride, ride, side, slide, snide, stride, tide, wide

big, dig, fig, gig, jig, pig, rig, sprig, twig, wig

blight, bright, fight, flight, fright, knight, light, might, night, plight, right, sight, slight, tight

brim, dim, grim, him, prim, rim, slim, swim, trim, vim, whim

MORE . . .

bill, chill, dill, drill, fill, frill, gill, grill, hill, ill, kill, mill, pill, quill, sill, skill, spill, still, thrill, twill, will

chime, crime, dime, grime, lime, prime, slime, time

bin, chin, din, fin, gin, grin, kin, pin, shin, sin, skin, spin, thin, tin, twin, win

bind, blind, find, grind, hind, kind, mind, rind, wind

brine, dine, fine, line, mine, nine, pine, shine, shrine, spine, swine, tine, vine, whine, wine

bing, bring, cling, ding, fling, king, ping, ring, sing, sling, spring, sting, string, swing, thing, wing, wring, zing

blink, brink, clink, drink, kink, link, mink, pink, rink, shrink, sink, stink, think, wink

flint, glint, hint, lint, mint, print, splint, sprint, squint, stint, tint

chip, clip, dip, drip, flip, grip, hip, lip, nip, quip, rip, ship, sip, skip, slip, snip, strip, tip, trip, whip, zip

bit, fit, flit, grit, hit, kit, knit, lit, pit, quit, sit, skit, slit, spit, split, wit

bite, kite, mite, quite, rite, site, spite, white, write

chive, dive, drive, five, hive, jive, live, strive, thrive

blob, cob, gob, job, knob, lob, mob, rob, slob, snob, sob

block, clock, crock, dock, flock, frock, hock, knock, lock, mock, rock, shock, smock, sock, stock, tock

clod, cod, mod, nod, plod, pod, prod, rod, shod, sod, trod

bog, clog, cog, flog, fog, frog, grog, hog, jog, log, smog, tog

broke, choke, coke, joke, poke, smoke, spoke, stoke, stroke, woke

bold, cold, fold, gold, hold, mold, old, scold, sold, told

bone, clone, cone, drone, hone, lone, phone, prone, stone, tone, zone

bong, dong, gong, long, prong, song, strong, thong, tong, wrong

MORE . . .

bop, chop, cop, crop, drop, flop, hop, mop, plop, pop, prop, shop, slop, sop, stop, top

cope, dope, grope, hope, lope, mope, nope, pope, rope, scope, slope

bore, chore, core, fore, gore, more, pore, score, shore, sore, spore, store, swore, tore, wore

born, corn, horn, morn, scorn, shorn, sworn, thorn, torn, worn

blot, clot, cot, got, hot, jot, knot, lot, not, plot, pot, rot, shot, slot, spot, tot, trot

blow, flow, glow, know, low, row, show, slow, snow, stow, tow

bow, brow, chow, cow, how, now, plow, row, scow, sow, vow, wow

bub, club, cub, dub, flub, grub, hub, nub, pub, rub, scrub, shrub, snub, stub, sub, tub

buck, cluck, duck, huck, luck, muck, pluck, puck, shuck, struck, stuck, suck, truck, tuck

bluff, buff, cuff, fluff, gruff, muff, puff, scuff, snuff, stuff

bug, chug, drug, dug, hug, jug, lug, mug, plug, pug, rug, shrug, slug, smug, snug, thug, tug

bum, chum, drum, glum, gum, hum, mum, plum, rum, scum, slum, strum, sum, swum, yum

bump, chump, clump, dump, frump, grump, hump, jump, lump, plump, pump, rump, slump, stump, sump, trump

bun, fun, gun, nun, pun, run, shun, spun, stun, sun

clung, flung, hung, lung, rung, slung, sprung, strung, stung, sung, swung, wrung

bunk, chunk, drunk, dunk, flunk, funk, hunk, junk, plunk, punk, shrunk, skunk, slunk, spunk, stunk, sunk, thunk, trunk

blush, brush, crush, flush, gush, hush, lush, mush, plush, rush, slush, thrush

but, cut, glut, gut, hut, jut, nut, rut, shut, smut, strut

by, cry, dry, fly, fry, my, ply, pry, shy, sky, sly, spy, try

MORE ABOUT SPELLING RULES

Very few spelling rules, or generalizations, are productive to teach. For a rule to be valid, it must apply to a large number of words and have few exceptions. Following are rules that meet this criteria.

SUFFIXES

Double the Final Consonant

Double the final consonant before adding a suffix that begins with the vowel to a word that ends with a single vowel-consonant. (get/getting)

Double the final consonant before adding a suffix that begins with a vowel to a word that is accented on the final syllable and ends with a single vowel-consonant. (permit/permitted)

Words Ending in Silent e

Drop the final e before adding a suffix that begins with a vowel. (have/having)

Keep the final e when adding a suffix that begins with a consonant. (late/lately)

Words Ending in y

Change the y to i when adding a suffix to words that end in consonant-y unless the suffix begins with i. (try/tried)

Do not change the y to i when adding a suffix to words that end in a vowel-y. (play/played)

PLURALS

Add s to most nouns to form plurals. (friend/friends)

Add es to nouns ending with s, ss, sh, ch, or x. (box/boxes, class/classes)

Change the y to i and add es to nouns ending in consonant-y. (country/countries)

Add s to nouns ending with vowel-y. (key/keys)

Change the f or fe to v and add es to some nouns ending in f or fe. (half/halves, knife/knives)

Some nouns change their spellings to make the plural. (foot/feet)

Some nouns are spelled the same for both singular and plural. (sheep)

One kind of homonym is a homophone. Homophones are words that are pronounced the same, but are spelled differently and have different meanings. Because of regional differences in pronunciation, what is or isn't a homophone often differs. Let's simply say, homophones are words that often sound the same, or nearly the same, when they are said. Homophones present a persistent spelling problem. The problem is more accurately described as a "usage" problem and will be addressed under the umbrella of "spelling in context."

Generally, teach homophones as sets making the focus of the lesson the distinction between (or among) the meanings and spellings of the sound-alike words. Teaching homophones as sets is appropriate when the words are already in the students' vocabulary. Also teach the homophones as sets if a member of the set may not be in the students' vocabulary, but could be introduced for vocabulary development. The homophones should not be taught as a set if a member of the set is a word that students would rarely, if ever, need at this point in their language use.

<u>Examples:</u>

Teach **be** and **bee** together because both words are in the students' everyday vocabulary.

Teach **very** and **vary** together because vary may be useful to add to the vocabulary of students.

Do not teach **great** and **grate** as sets because **grate** would probably not be a useful word to developing writers. Instead, treat **great** as a regular word rather than as a homophone when it is initially introduced.

Following are resources for further homophone study:

How Ships Play Cards: A Beginning Book of Homonyms
    Cynthia Basil; Morrow, 1980; Grades 1-3
A Scale Full of Fish and Other Turnabouts
    Naomi Bossom; Greenwillow, 1979; Grades 1-3
Your Ant Is a Which: Fun With Homophones
    Bernice Hunt; Harcourt, 1976; Grades 3-6
Eight Ate: A Feast of Homonym Riddles
    Marvin Terban; Houghton, 1982; Grades 2-4
Two-Way Words
    Imbior Kudrna; Abingdon Press, 1980; Grades 1-4
The King Who Reigned
    Fred Gwynne; Prentice-Hall, 1970; Grades 3-8
    (Also by the same author: *The Sixteen Hand Horse and A Chocolate Moose For Dinner*)
Hey, Hay!: A Wagonful of Funny Homonym Riddles
    Marvin Terban; Clarion, 1991; Grades 4-8

MORE...

Following are examples of <u>high-frequency homophones</u>:

accept/except	I <u>accept</u> your invitation to dinner. Everyone is here, <u>except</u> Bob.
ad/add	I saw the <u>ad</u> in the newspaper. <u>Add</u> 2+2 to get 4.
addition/edition	The math quiz tested <u>addition</u> and subtraction. This is a new <u>edition</u> of the book.
affect/effect	The vote will <u>affect</u> our final decision. The rain has an <u>effect</u> on plant growth.
ail/ale	Your leg will <u>ail</u> you until it heals. It is better to drink milk than <u>ale</u>.
air/err/heir	Breathe the fresh <u>air</u>. To <u>err</u>, or make a mistake, is human. The prince was the <u>heir</u> to the throne.
aisle/I'll/isle	The bride walked down the <u>aisle</u>. <u>I'll</u> do my homework before dinner. He vacations on an <u>isle</u> in the Pacific Ocean.
all/awl	We have <u>all</u> the books and they have none. The carpenter uses a tool called an <u>awl</u>.
aloud/allowed	Read the message <u>aloud</u> so everyone can hear. No bikes are <u>allowed</u> on the sidewalk.
altar/alter	The bride and groom stood at the <u>altar</u>. I must <u>alter</u> this skirt to make it fit.
ant/aunt	A small <u>ant</u> crawled across the log. My <u>aunt</u> and uncle are coming to visit us.
arc/ark	An <u>arc</u> of light filled the sky. Noah and the animals sailed on the <u>ark</u>.
ascent/assent	Our <u>ascent</u> to the top of the hill was slow. She gave her <u>assent</u> to our plan.
assistance/assistants	Teachers provide <u>assistance</u> to students. The doctor had two <u>assistants</u> to help her.
ate/eight	I <u>ate</u> a sandwich for lunch. The girl was <u>eight</u> years old.
attendance/ attendants	He never missed school so his <u>attendance</u> record was good. The zoo has two <u>attendants</u> to watch the animals.

68

MORE . . .

aural/oral	An <u>aural</u> exam may discover a hearing problem. An <u>oral</u> exam may tell us why she has a toothache.
away/aweigh	The bird flew <u>away</u>. The ship's crew yelled, "Anchors <u>aweigh</u>!"
aye/eye/I	All those in favor say <u>aye</u>. Cover one <u>eye</u> and then try to read this. <u>I</u> like to play baseball.
bail/bale	<u>Bail</u> the water out of the boat before it sinks. The farmer sat to rest on a <u>bale</u> of hay.
ball/bawl	Throw the <u>ball</u> to me. He will <u>bawl</u> big tears if he doesn't get his way.
balm/bomb	Skin <u>balm</u> makes skin smooth. The <u>bomb</u> exploded in fire.
band/banned	The <u>band</u> played a song everyone knew. Dogs not on a leash are <u>banned</u> from the park.
bard/barred	The actor played a <u>bard</u> reading funny poems. The woman <u>barred</u> the door so no one could enter.
baron/barren	The man was known as an oil <u>baron</u> in his state. The land was dry and <u>barren</u>.
bare/bear	He walked in his <u>bare</u> feet carrying his shoes. The <u>bear</u> had thick, brown fur.
base/bass	The house was down at the <u>base</u> of the mountain. He sang <u>bass</u> in the school choir.
basis/bases	The decision is made on the <u>basis</u> of the vote. The batter ran around the <u>bases</u> to home plate.
be/bee	It will <u>be</u> late before we reach home. The honey <u>bee</u> buzzed around the flower.
beach/beech	The children played in the sand at the <u>beach</u>. We have a tall <u>beech</u> tree in our yard.
beat/beet	The drummer <u>beat</u> the drum. She sliced a <u>beet</u> to put in the salad.
beau/bow	The girl and her <u>beau</u> danced at the party. She wore a red <u>bow</u> in her hair.
been/bin	He has not <u>been</u> feeling well. There is flour in the <u>bin</u> to make the bread.

MORE . . .

bell/belle	The school <u>bell</u> rang. The beautiful lady was the <u>belle</u> of the ball.
berry/bury	She made a <u>berry</u> pie for dessert. Watch the dog <u>bury</u> the bone.
berth/birth	He slept in a <u>berth</u> on the ship. We watched the <u>birth</u> of the birds as each egg hatched.
better/bettor	This book is <u>better</u> than that one. The <u>bettor</u> placed a bet on the racehorse.
billed/build	The company <u>billed</u> us for their services. See the child <u>build</u> a tower with the blocks.
bite/byte	The dog looks mean, but he won't <u>bite</u>. The computer processes an 8-bit <u>byte</u>.
blew/blue	The wind <u>blew</u> the leaves off the trees. The sky was <u>blue</u> without one cloud in it.
boar/bore	The <u>boar</u> was in the pig pen. Slow ball games often <u>bore</u> me.
board/bored	He hammered a nail into the <u>board</u>. He became <u>bored</u> with the movie and fell asleep.
boarder/border	The boarding house had a room for another <u>boarder</u>. A <u>border</u> of red blooms surrounded the flower bed.
bolder/boulder	The king was <u>bolder</u> and more courageous than the prince. The <u>boulder</u> was so large we could not move it.
borough/burro/burrow	The people of this <u>borough</u> will vote today. The <u>burro</u> packed the equipment up the mountain. Watch the animal <u>burrow</u> a hole in the ground.
bough/bow	One <u>bough</u> of the tree had more blooms than the others. The captain stood at the <u>bow</u> of the ship. The audience clapped as the actor took a <u>bow</u>.
bouillon/bullion	The sick child drank warm <u>bouillon</u>. Put the silver and gold <u>bullion</u> in the safe.
brake/break	<u>Brake</u> the car to slow the speed. The egg will <u>break</u> if it drops from the nest.
bread/bred	I used fresh <u>bread</u> to make my sandwich. The mare was <u>bred</u> in hopes of getting a colt.
brewed/brood	She <u>brewed</u> a pot of tea. The <u>brood</u> of chicks followed the hen.

MORE . . . .

brews/bruise	She <u>brews</u> tea every morning. I got this <u>bruise</u> on my leg when I fell.
bridal/bridle	The bride and groom danced at the <u>bridal</u> party. Put the <u>bridle</u> on the horse.
buy/by/bye	I'll <u>buy</u> groceries for dinner at the store. The book was written <u>by</u> the boy standing by the door. The baby waved "<u>bye</u>."
callous/callus	She is a <u>callous</u> person, not kind and forgiving. The long walk made a painful <u>callus</u> on his foot.
canvas/canvass	The tent was made of heavy <u>canvas</u>. The police will <u>canvass</u> the town for the robber.
capital/capitol	Austin is the <u>capital</u> of Texas. Begin each sentence with a <u>capital</u> letter. Her office is in the <u>capitol</u> building.
carat/caret/carrot	She wore a diamond weighing one <u>carat</u>. The editor used a <u>caret</u> to add a word to the sentence. The horse wanted to eat the orange <u>carrot</u>.
carol/carrel	"Silent Night" is his favorite Christmas <u>carol</u>. A <u>carrel</u> in the library is a quiet place to study.
caught/cot	The mice <u>caught</u> the cat in the funny story. She slept on the <u>cot</u> in the tent.
ceiling/sealing	Water dripped through the <u>ceiling</u>. She is <u>sealing</u> the envelopes before mailing them.
cell/sell	The jail had only one <u>cell</u> for a prisoner. We will <u>sell</u> this car and buy another one.
cellar/seller	It's cool on a hot day down in the <u>cellar</u>. The <u>seller</u> and the buyer signed a sales contract.
censor/sensor	If they <u>censor</u> this book, we cannot read it in school. The <u>sensor</u> turns the light on when noise is sensed.
census/senses	A <u>census</u> gives us population information. One of our <u>senses</u> is our eyes.
cent/scent/sent	One <u>cent</u> is one penny. The room was filled with the <u>scent</u> of roses. I <u>sent</u> a letter to you.
cents/scents/sense	It costs ten <u>cents</u>. The <u>scents</u> I like best are flower fragrances. Use common <u>sense</u> to decide when to come home.

MORE....

cereal/serial	She eats <u>cereal</u> for breakfast. The <u>serial</u> number is on the back.
chalk/chock	He writes on the chalkboard with <u>chalk</u>. <u>Chock</u> the car's wheels so it won't roll down the hill.
cheap/cheep	The price was <u>cheap</u>, not expensive. The baby chick chirped a little <u>cheep</u> sound.
chews/choose	The dog <u>chews</u> on the steak bone. What color ribbon will you <u>choose</u>?
choral/coral	The <u>choral</u> groups sang the songs together. The <u>coral</u> in the ocean is a <u>coral</u> color.
chord/cord	The teacher played a <u>chord</u> on the piano. I tied the box with strong <u>cord</u>.
chute/shoot	The clothes fell through the laundry <u>chute</u>. The gun would not <u>shoot</u>.
cite/sight/site	I can <u>cite</u> evidence to prove I'm right. The plane disappeared out of <u>sight</u>. This land is the <u>site</u> for our new park.
claws/clause	The cat had sharp <u>claws</u>. One <u>clause</u> in the contract was on pay raises.
close/clothes	Please <u>close</u> the door as you go out. Hang your <u>clothes</u> in this closet.
coarse/course	The sandpaper was <u>coarse</u>, not fine. Of <u>course</u>, I will be there. He enrolled in a college history <u>course</u>.
colonel/kernel	The <u>colonel</u> took orders from the general. One <u>kernel</u> of corn fell to the floor.
complement/ compliment	This picture will <u>complement</u> your room. I'd like to <u>compliment</u> you on your fine work.
coop/coupe	Feed the chickens in the chicken <u>coop</u>. The new car is a <u>coupe</u>, not a sedan.
core/corps	Throw the apple <u>core</u> into the trash. The army <u>corps</u> had their meeting today.
correspondence/ correspondents	The secretary handles the office <u>correspondence</u>. Writers may be <u>correspondents</u> for magazines.
council/counsel	The president's <u>council</u> has its meeting today. Teachers <u>counsel</u> students to help solve their problems.

MORE . . .

creak/creek	Listen to my shoes <u>creak</u> when I walk. The children play in the <u>creek</u> on hot days.
crews/cruise/cruse	The road <u>crews</u> sanded the snowy streets. See the ship <u>cruise</u> slowly by the island. Pour the oil slowly from the <u>cruse</u>.
cue/queue	Give me a <u>cue</u> when I'm to begin singing. The <u>queue</u> to buy tickets is a block long.
currant/current	The <u>currant</u> she ate looked like a tiny raisin. The <u>current</u> time is 4:30 PM.
cymbal/symbol	The <u>cymbal</u> made a musical ringing sound. Our flag is a <u>symbol</u> of American freedom.
days/daze	Summer <u>days</u> are warm and sunny. The blow to his head put him into a <u>daze</u>.
dear/deer	She is a <u>dear</u> child. The herd of <u>deer</u> ran into the forest.
dew/do/due	The <u>dew</u> on the grass made my feet wet. What <u>do</u> you want to do today? My library book is <u>due</u>.
dense/dents	The forest is <u>dense</u> with trees. After the crash, the car had many <u>dents</u>.
desert/dessert	True fans won't <u>desert</u> the team if it loses. There was apple pie for <u>dessert</u>.
die/dye	The plant will <u>die</u> without water. <u>Dye</u> the shoes a color to match your dress.
doe/dough	The <u>doe</u> followed the other deer into the woods. The <u>dough</u> will make a big loaf of bread.
done/dun	I'll be home as soon as the work is <u>done</u>. The store will <u>dun</u> him until he pays his bill.
dual/duel	The car had <u>dual</u> exhaust pipes, rather than just one. The two men will <u>duel</u> to see who marries the princess.
earn/urn	I'll <u>earn</u> more money on my new job. The <u>urn</u> contained a bouquet of flowers.
epic/epoch	The literature teacher assigned an <u>epic</u> to read. The earth began a new <u>epoch</u> when space travel began.
ewe/yew/you	The <u>ewe</u> stood by her lamb. They planted a <u>yew</u> tree in the park. It's time for <u>you</u> to eat dinner.

MORE . . .

exercise/exorcise	Walking is good <u>exercise</u>. They'll <u>exorcise</u> the demon at the end of the story.
eyelet/islet	The blouse had a decorated <u>eyelet</u> on each pocket. There was a small <u>islet</u> next to the big island.
faint/feint	Even a <u>faint</u> sound will make the lady faint. The boxer will <u>feint</u> a jab and then deliver a real one.
fairy/ferry	I put my tooth under my pillow for the tooth <u>fairy</u>. We took the <u>ferry</u> boat across the river.
fair/fare	Divide the money in a way that is <u>fair</u> to all. The state <u>fair</u> is in August. Bus <u>fare</u> is fifty cents.
feat/feet	The magician will attempt a remarkable <u>feat</u>. My <u>feet</u> have grown too big for these shoes.
find/fined	I'm sure you'll <u>find</u> your lost gloves soon. The driver was <u>fined</u> for speeding.
fir/fur	There is a tall <u>fir</u> tree in the park. The <u>fur</u> on our cat is soft and smooth.
flair/flare	She has a <u>flair</u> for decorating. Place the <u>flare</u> in the road to warn oncoming cars.
flea/flee	The dog wears a <u>flea</u> collar because it has fleas. The robber tried to <u>flee</u> after the robbery.
flew/flu/flue	The bird <u>flew</u> up to the nest. I'm sick in bed with the <u>flu</u>. Open the chimney <u>flue</u> before you light the fire.
flour/flower	The recipe calls for four cups of <u>flour</u>. My favorite <u>flower</u> is the rose.
for/fore/four	The letter is <u>for</u> you. The golfer yelled, "<u>Fore</u>!" There are <u>four</u> letters in the word "<u>four</u>."
foreword/forward	Read the <u>foreword</u> of the book for the author's notes. The winners stepped <u>forward</u> to get their prizes.
forth/fourth	They lived happily from that day <u>forth</u>. Independence Day is on the <u>fourth</u> day of July.
foul/fowl	There was a <u>foul</u> smell to the spoiled meat. The pond was the home for fish and <u>fowl</u>.
gait/gate	The horse trotted at a fast <u>gait</u>. The <u>gate</u> to the fenced yard was locked.

MORE . . . .

genes/jeans	Your <u>genes</u> determine your eye color. The <u>jeans</u> faded to light blue in the wash.
grate/great	Build the fire on the fireplace <u>grate</u>. America is a <u>great</u> country!
grease/Greece	The engine had black <u>grease</u> on it. <u>Greece</u> is a country.
groan/grown	Do not <u>groan</u> about having homework to do. The child has <u>grown</u> an inch taller.
guessed/guest	She <u>guessed</u> at the answer. Please be my <u>guest</u> for dinner tonight.
hail/hale	The <u>hail</u> covered the ground like snow. "<u>Hail</u> to the chief!" the crowd roared. The old man is <u>hale</u> and active.
hair/hare	Her hat covered her <u>hair</u>. The <u>hare</u> hopped into the woods.
hall/haul	The bedrooms are down the <u>hall</u>. We will <u>haul</u> the trash away in the truck.
hay/hey	The barn was full of <u>hay</u>. <u>Hey</u>, you! Stop!
heal/heel/he'll	The medicine will help the sore to <u>heal</u>. The <u>heel</u> on the shoe fell off. <u>He'll</u> help you carry the large box.
hear/here	Listen to <u>hear</u> the phone ring. Come <u>here</u>.
heard/herd	She <u>heard</u> the dog bark at the stranger. There is a large <u>herd</u> of cattle on the range.
hi/high	The girl shook hands and said, "<u>Hi</u>." The moon is <u>high</u> in the night sky.
higher/hire	No mountain is <u>higher</u> than Mt. Everest. They will <u>hire</u> another worker for the job.
him/hymn	Give the book to <u>him</u>, not her. The <u>hymn</u> is on page five of the song book.
hoarse/horse	My voice is <u>hoarse</u> after cheering for the team. Ride the <u>horse</u> into the barn.
hoes/hose	He <u>hoes</u> the garden soil. The fire fighter held the fire <u>hose</u>.

MORE....

hole/whole	There is a <u>hole</u> in my old blue jeans. I ate the <u>whole</u> cake by myself!
hour/our	Sixty minutes make one <u>hour</u>. We move into <u>our</u> new house this week.
in/inn	Come <u>in</u> out of the rain. We spent the night at the <u>inn</u>.
its/it's	The dog went round chasing <u>its</u> tail. <u>It's</u> going to rain today.
knead/need	<u>Knead</u> the bread dough to make it smooth. The plant will <u>need</u> water to grow.
knew/new	The student <u>knew</u> the answers to the test questions. My <u>new</u> shoes hurt my feet.
knight/night	The <u>knight</u> rode to the castle on his horse. The moon shines in the sky at <u>night</u>.
knot/not	Tie a <u>knot</u> in the rope. Dinner is <u>not</u> ready yet.
know/no	I did not <u>know</u> her name. <u>No</u>, I will not be late for work.
knows/nose	She <u>knows</u> how to fly a plane. Breathe air through your <u>nose</u>.
lead/led	I broke the <u>lead</u> of my pencil. He <u>led</u> the horse along the trail.
leader/liter	Our president is our <u>leader</u>. The jar contains one <u>liter</u> of water.
leak/leek	Water will <u>leak</u> through the hole in the roof. Mother made <u>leek</u> soup for dinner.
lessen/lesson	I can <u>lessen</u> your load by carrying this bag. The teacher explained the math <u>lesson</u>.
lie/lye	Do not tell a <u>lie</u> to your father. <u>Lye</u> can be used to make soap.
loan/lone	The bank gave me a <u>loan</u> to buy the car. The <u>lone</u> wolf must have left the pack.
made/maid	She <u>made</u> sandwiches for lunch. The <u>maid</u> washed the clothes.
mail/male	Put the <u>mail</u> in the post office mailbox. Dad is a <u>male</u>, not a female.

MORE . . .

main/Maine/mane	This is the <u>main</u> road into the city. The man is from the state of <u>Maine</u>. Brush the horse's <u>mane</u> until it is smooth.
manner/manor	She spoke to me in an unkind <u>manner</u>. The family lives in the <u>manor</u> on the hill.
marry/merry	Will you <u>marry</u> me? The people sang and were <u>merry</u> at the party.
meat/meet	We will roast the <u>meat</u> for dinner. Let's <u>meet</u> at the clock tower in the park.
might/mite	If it gets colder, it <u>might</u> snow. There is a tiny <u>mite</u> on the leaf.
mind/mined	I have a good idea on my <u>mind</u>. They <u>mined</u> silver from the Kellogg Mine.
miner/minor	The <u>miner</u> used special tools for his work. The child was a <u>minor</u> and not old enough to vote. The problem was only <u>minor</u>, not major.
missed/mist	He <u>missed</u> four answers on the test. She <u>missed</u> her friend who moved away. Soon the <u>mist</u> turned to heavy rain.
moose/mousse	A <u>moose</u> is larger than a deer. She made a chocolate <u>mousse</u> for dessert.
none/nun	I ate them all and have <u>none</u> left. The <u>nun</u> sang in the church choir.
oar/or/ore	There is only one <u>oar</u> in the boat. I will choose either red <u>or</u> blue. The <u>ore</u> comes from the mine.
oh/owe	<u>Oh</u>, what a surprise! I <u>owe</u> her three dollars.
one/won	There is <u>one</u> capital city in each state. Our team <u>won</u> the ball game.
overdo/overdue	If you <u>overdo</u>, you'll be too tired. There's a fine on all <u>overdue</u> library books.
overseas/oversees	We plan to sail <u>overseas</u> this summer. The teacher <u>oversees</u> the students' work.
paced/paste	She <u>paced</u> back and forth as she waited. Use <u>paste</u> or glue to make it stick.

MORE . . .

packed/pact	She <u>packed</u> her suitcase. The scouts made a <u>pact</u> of friendship.
pail/pale	He carried the water in the <u>pail</u>. The dark blue jeans turned <u>pale</u> blue in the wash.
pain/pane	The <u>pain</u> of a toothache hurts. The glass was from the broken window <u>pane</u>.
pair/pare/pear	I have a new <u>pair</u> of shoes. <u>Pare</u> the potatoes before you boil them. She wanted an apple or a <u>pear</u> to eat.
passed/past	The marching band played loudly as they <u>passed</u>. The <u>past</u> is recorded in our history books.
patience/patients	Making the quilt required much <u>patience</u> and skill. The nurse cared for the sick <u>patients</u>.
pause/paws	A comma tells your voice to <u>pause</u> as you read. The cat licked its front <u>paws</u> to clean them.
peace/piece	<u>Peace</u> followed the war. I ate a <u>piece</u> of candy.
peak/peek	The mountain is 11,000 feet at its highest <u>peak</u>. Close your eyes and do not <u>peek</u>.
peal/peel	I slipped on a banana <u>peal</u>. The bells <u>peel</u> at noon.
pedal/peddle	It's hard to <u>pedal</u> the bike uphill. The sales people <u>peddle</u> their goods to buyers.
plain/plane	I want <u>plain</u> vanilla, nothing fancy. The cattle roam on the <u>plain</u>. The pilot landed the <u>plane</u> at the airport.
pole/poll	The flag waves at the top of the <u>pole</u>. The results of the <u>poll</u> determine the winner.
pore/pour	A <u>pore</u> of my skin is too small to see. Please <u>pour</u> the milk into the glass.
praise/prays/preys	I will <u>praise</u> her for doing a fine job. She <u>prays</u> at the church. The cat <u>preys</u> on the mouse.
presence/presents	She felt the <u>presence</u> of a ghost at the haunted house. Guests brought <u>presents</u> to the birthday party.
prince/prints	The <u>prince</u> lives in the castle. See the foot <u>prints</u> in the snow.

MORE ...

principal/principle	The <u>principal</u> called a teachers' meeting. One <u>principle</u> I live by is, "Be kind to animals."
profit/prophet	The children made ten cents <u>profit</u> on each lemonade sold. The <u>prophet</u> taught the meaning of the Bible.
prophecy/prophesy	What is the astrologer's <u>prophecy</u> for the future? Can an astrologer <u>prophesy</u> the future?
quarts/quartz	Buy two <u>quarts</u> of milk at the grocery store. The ring had a <u>quartz</u> stone.
rain/reign/rein	The <u>rain</u> made big puddles on the streets. We studied the twenty-year <u>reign</u> of the king. Hold tightly each <u>rein</u> of the horse's bridle.
raise/rays/raze	<u>Raise</u> the window shade so we can see outside. The <u>rays</u> of the sun may burn your skin. The wrecking crew will <u>raze</u> the building.
read/reed	The boy will learn to <u>read</u> in school. Each green <u>reed</u> grew tall in the swamp.
read/red	I <u>read</u> the book yesterday. The cars stopped when the traffic light turned <u>red</u>.
real/reel	The story is <u>real</u>, not make-believe. He has his fishing <u>reel</u> and his pole.
residence/residents	Their <u>residence</u> is the white house on Maple Street. The <u>residents</u> of the new apartments can move in today.
review/revue	To prepare for the test, I <u>review</u> my notes. The actor in tonight's <u>revue</u> is practicing his part.
right/rite/write	There were four <u>right</u> and one wrong on my test. Cars drive on the <u>right</u> side of the road. The dance is part of an old Native American <u>rite</u>. <u>Write</u> down your name at the top of the paper.
ring/wring	Draw a <u>ring</u> around the answer. <u>Wring</u> the water from the cloth.
road/rode/rowed	We live at the end of this dirt <u>road</u>. She <u>rode</u> her horse in the rodeo. They <u>rowed</u> the boat across the lake.
role/roll	He played the <u>role</u> of the king in the play. The dog will <u>roll</u> over to earn a treat. He ate a hot <u>roll</u> with his dinner.

MORE...

root/route	The <u>root</u> of the plant was below the ground. We <u>root</u> for the home team to win. There is little traffic on the <u>route</u> I drive home.
rose/rows	A <u>rose</u> is my favorite flower. The sun <u>rose</u> overhead as noon approached. They planted ten <u>rows</u> of corn in the garden.
rote/wrote	I know the poem so well I say it by <u>rote</u>. She <u>wrote</u> and mailed the letter.
rung/wrung	She climbed each <u>rung</u> of the ladder. He <u>wrung</u> the water from the cloth.
sail/sale	The <u>sail</u> on the sailboat caught the wind. All <u>sale</u> items are marked below the original price.
scene/seen	The artist painted a <u>scene</u> of hills and lakes. I haven't <u>seen</u> a movie in a long time.
sea/see	Columbus sailed across the <u>sea</u> to the new land. It is hard to <u>see</u> well in the dark.
seas/sees/seize	The <u>seas</u> are in blue on the maps. He <u>sees</u> better with his glasses. The big dog will <u>seize</u> the bone from the little dog.
seam/seem	Stitch along the <u>seam</u> to fix the tear in your shirt. She does not <u>seem</u> to be very happy.
sew/so/sow	I need a needle and thread to <u>sew</u>. It's raining, <u>so</u> I'll wear my raincoat. The farmer will <u>sow</u> the seeds in the spring.
shear/sheer	<u>Shear</u> the plants to a height of six inches. I can see through this <u>sheer</u> material.
shoe/shoo	The toe of my left <u>shoe</u> is too tight. <u>Shoo</u> the flies away from the food!
shone/shown	The hot sun <u>shone</u> brightly. The young campers were <u>shown</u> how to start the campfire.
side/sighed	Walk on the left <u>side</u> of the road. She <u>sighed</u> with relief when the ball missed the window.
soar/sore	Watch the eagle <u>soar</u> through the sky. My throat is too <u>sore</u> to swallow.
sole/soul	There is a hole in the <u>sole</u> of my shoe. She is the <u>sole</u> survivor of the accident. May his <u>soul</u> rest in peace.

MORE . . .

some/sum	<u>Some</u> people like to swim, while others do not. The <u>sum</u> of "two plus two" is four.
son/sun	The man had a <u>son</u> and a daughter. Most plants grow best with light from the <u>sun</u>.
stairs/stares	Hold the handrail as you climb the <u>stairs</u>. The child <u>stares</u> at the picture on the TV.
stake/steak	The wooden <u>stake</u> in the ground marks the spot. She fried a <u>steak</u> for dinner.
stationary/stationery	The exercise bike was <u>stationary</u>. The <u>stationery</u> had matching envelopes.
steal/steel	Robbers <u>steal</u> things from others. The strong bridge was made of <u>steel</u>.
step/steppe	Watch your <u>step</u>. A <u>steppe</u> is a great plain with few trees.
straight/strait	Stand up <u>straight</u> while I measure your height. The ship sailed through the narrow <u>strait</u>.
suede/swayed	The jacket is made of <u>suede</u> leather. The tree <u>swayed</u> in the wind.
suite/sweet	The bedroom <u>suite</u> had four matching furniture pieces. The candy tasted <u>sweet</u>.
summary/summery	A book report may be a <u>summary</u> of the story. The <u>summery</u> weather was a change from the cold.
sundae/Sunday	He had an ice cream <u>sundae</u> for dessert. We're going to Grandma's on <u>Sunday</u>.
tacks/tax	The <u>tacks</u> held the picture in place on the wall. There is a <u>tax</u> on all food sold.
tail/tale	A squirrel has a long <u>tail</u>. The teacher read us a <u>tale</u> from the storybook.
taught/taut	The coach <u>taught</u> the team how to play the ball game. The rope is already <u>taut</u> without tightening it.
tea/tee	The meal was served with <u>tea</u> or coffee. The golfer stepped up to the <u>tee</u> to hit the ball.
team/teem	The <u>team</u> that earns the most points wins. The buzzing bees <u>teem</u> around the beehive.
teas/tease/tees	There are several kinds of Chinese <u>teas</u>. Do not <u>tease</u> your younger sister. Golfers hit their balls from golf <u>tees</u>.

MORE...

their/there/they're	We are going to <u>their</u> house for dinner. The book is over <u>there</u> on the table. <u>They're</u> listening to the music.
theirs/there's	That car is <u>theirs</u>. <u>There's</u> something inside the box.
threw/through	He <u>threw</u> the ball to his friend. I am <u>through</u> with my homework. She climbed <u>through</u> the window.
throne/thrown	Queen Anna sat at her <u>throne</u> in the castle. The baseball was <u>thrown</u> to first base.
thyme/time	<u>Thyme</u> is a plant used to flavor food. What <u>time</u> does the clock say?
tide/tied	The <u>tide</u> brought the sea up high on the shore. She <u>tied</u> a ribbon in her hair.
to/too/two	I go <u>to</u> school on the bus. They are going home, <u>too</u>. They ran <u>too</u> fast for me to keep up with them. The airplane has <u>two</u> wings.
toad/towed	The green <u>toad</u> hopped into the pond. The car was <u>towed</u> to the gas station to get fixed.
toe/tow	He stepped on my <u>toe</u> when we danced. They will <u>tow</u> the car to the garage.
told/tolled	The teacher <u>told</u> the class the answer. The bell <u>tolled</u> twelve times at midnight.
vain/vane/vein	The <u>vain</u> prince looked into the mirror. The weather <u>vane</u> on the roof turned with the wind. A <u>vein</u> carries blood back to our heart.
vary/very	The children <u>vary</u> in size from small to large. It is <u>very</u> cold today.
wade/weighed	Take your shoes off before you <u>wade</u> in the stream. I <u>weighed</u> myself on the scale.
waist/waste	I tied the belt around my <u>waist</u>. Do not <u>waste</u> the colored paper.
wait/weight	<u>Wait</u> in front of the school for your ride. She lost <u>weight</u> on her diet.
way/weigh	I do not remember the <u>way</u> to his house. I <u>weigh</u> 100 pounds.

MORE . . .

war/wore	The soldier fought in the <u>war</u>. He <u>wore</u> a red hat.
ware/wear/where	The <u>ware</u> in the pottery shop is for sale. <u>Wear</u> your best clothes to the party. I do not know <u>where</u> they went.
wave/waive	<u>Wave</u> good-bye to the people as they leave. He will <u>waive</u> the rule, as it is not a good one.
we/wee	<u>We</u> are going shopping. The elf wore a <u>wee</u> little green cap.
weak/week	I'm too <u>weak</u> to lift the big box. There are seven days in one <u>week</u>.
weather/whether	The <u>weather</u> will be warm for the picnic. I don't know <u>whether</u> I can go.
weave/we've	<u>Weave</u> the yarn together to make the material. <u>We've</u> been gone on vacation.
we'd/weed	<u>We'd</u> be interested in hearing about your trip. He dug the <u>weed</u> from the flower bed.
which/witch	I don't know <u>which</u> answer is the right one. The make-believe <u>witch</u> wore a tall, black hat.
who's/whose	<u>Who's</u> going to go with me? I don't know <u>whose</u> jacket this is.
wood/would	Bring in <u>wood</u> for the fire. She <u>would</u> like to help you.
yoke/yolk	The oxen were harnessed together with the <u>yoke</u>. The <u>yolk</u> of the egg is yellow.
you'll/yule	<u>You'll</u> have a birthday soon. The <u>yule</u> festival begins tonight.
your/you're	This is <u>your</u> book. <u>You're</u> a fast runner.

HOMOGRAPHS
+ HOMOPHONES
—————————
total = HOMONYMS

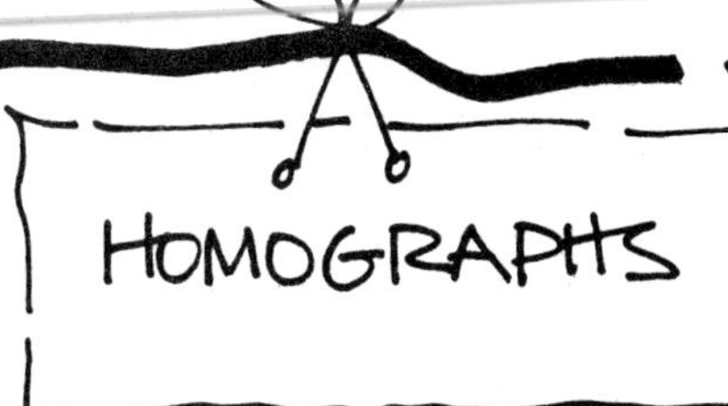

One kind of homonym is a homograph. Homographs are words that are pronounced differently, but are spelled the same and have different meanings. Homographs do not present the spelling problem that homophones present. Nonetheless, they can be explored for meaning and pronunciation if they are encountered in a spelling list.

Here are examples...

bass

He sings in a low <u>bass</u> voice.
We fish for <u>bass</u>.

conduct

Your everyday <u>conduct</u> determines your behavior grade.
He will <u>conduct</u> the orchestra.

content

Part of our writing grade is for <u>content</u>.
I'm <u>content</u> now that I've eaten.

contest

Don't <u>contest</u> the decision.
The <u>contest</u> will determine the winner.

contract

The <u>contract</u> I signed cannot be broken.
He may <u>contract</u> the disease if he's exposed to it.

converse

At home they <u>converse</u> in Spanish.
The <u>converse</u> of small is big.

desert

The <u>desert</u> is sandy and hot.
Do not <u>desert</u> the group and go alone.

does

What <u>does</u> the sign say?
The <u>does</u> were with the fawns in the forest.

excuse

You need a written <u>excuse</u> when you're absent.
Please <u>excuse</u> me from the dinner table.

lead

The <u>lead</u> in my pencil broke.
The teacher will <u>lead</u> the way.

minute

Wait a <u>minute</u>.
The little doll wore a <u>minute</u> hat.

MORE . . .

object

> The unidentified flying <u>object</u> glowed in the sky.
> I <u>object</u> to your plan.

present

> I gave him a birthday <u>present</u>.
> She will <u>present</u> the award to the winner.

primer

> The first book in first grade is the <u>primer</u>.
> Put <u>primer</u> on the wall before you wallpaper.

purpose

> The <u>purpose</u> for the meeting is to elect officers.
> The mayor will <u>purpose</u> that a new bridge be built.

read

> Can you <u>read</u> this book?
> She <u>read</u> the directions aloud.

record

> He set a new scoring <u>record</u>.
> <u>Record</u> your voice on this tape.

refuse

> I <u>refuse</u> to go.
> Place the <u>refuse</u> in the trash can.

sow

> The farmer will <u>sow</u> the seeds in spring.
> A female pig is called a <u>sow</u>.

subject

> The <u>subject</u> of the story is lions.
> Don't <u>subject</u> me to this punishment.

tear

> Don't <u>tear</u> the paper.
> The sad clown had a <u>tear</u> in his eye.

use

> I'll make good <u>use</u> of this.
> <u>Use</u> this pencil to write.

wind

> The <u>wind</u> blew.
> <u>Wind</u> the string into a ball.

 What is a prefix?

A prefix is a small group of letters attached, or fixed, to the beginning of a base word or root. A prefix changes the meaning of the word. Knowing the meaning of prefixes is helpful in unlocking the meaning of a word that has a prefix.

Here are common prefixes, their meanings, with word examples...

a—(unstressed) on, in, full of...*aboard, afire, aflame, afoot, ashore, atop, amiss, afield, apart, aglow, awake, alive, along, aloft, await, asleep*

a, an—(usually stressed) not, without...*agraphia, anesthesia, amoral, anemia, anonymous, apathy, aperiodic, aphasia, anarchy, asocial, atheist, atrophy*

ab—from, away...*abstain, abstract, abnormal, abscess, abhor, abduct, aberrant, abject, absent, absorb, abuse, absolve, abscond*

ac, ad, af, ag, an, as—to...*acquire, accept, adhere, admit, afflict, affirm, aggravate, aggressive, announce, annex, aspire, assert, ascertain*

ambi, amphi—both, around...*ambiance, ambidextrous, ambivalent, ambiguous, ambiguity, ambition, ambient, amphibian, amphitheater*

ante—before, prior to...*anterior, antecedent, antenatal, antevert, antediluvian, antedate*

anti—against...*antiwar, antisocial, antinuclear, antibody, antifreeze, antidote, anticlimactic, antigen, antiseptic, antitrust*

auto—self...*automatic, automobile, autograph, autobiography, autocratic, autonomic, automat, automation, autosuggestion*

be—by, make, around...*belittle, beneath, become, bedazzle, beware, betray, before, befriend, beside, behalf, behead, behold, belated, between*

bene—good, well...*benediction, benefactor, beneficial, benefit, benevolence, benevolent, benign, benignant, benefice, beneficent*

bi—two...*biannual, bimonthly, biweekly, bicentennial, bilateral, biplane, bipartisan, biennial, biped, bilingual, bicycle*

MORE...

by—close by, near, side, secondary...*bygone, bypass, byplay, byproduct, byroad, bystreet, byway, bypath, byword, byline, byroad*

circu, circum—around...*circle, circulate, circumference, circumspect, circumstance, circus, circuit, circumvent, circuitous, circumscribe*

co, col, com, con—with, together...*collaborate, collect, condense, conform, construct, comply, consensus, connect, cooperate, copilot, compose, compile*

contra, counter—against, opposite...*contraband, contraception, contradict, contrary, contravene, counteract, counterclockwise, counterfeit, counterpoint*

dia—through, across, apart, between...*diagnosis, diagram, diagonal, dialect, dialogue, dialysis, diameter, diaphragm, diathermic, diatonic*

de, dis—from, down, away, not...*detour, degrade, deform, dethrone, depart, decode, demote, disappear, dismiss, disagree, disconnect, dishonest, disobey*

dys—bad...*dysentery, dyslexia, dyspepsia, dysphasia, dysfunctional, dysphonia, dysplasia, dystopia, dystrophy,*

e—out, away...*elect, elate, elapse, eclipse, erect, emotion, effuse, eject, evacuate, emerge, event, elicit, emollient, evade*

em, en—in, into, make, make into...*embed, embrace, embroider, embellish, embattle, encourage, enlarge, encase, enclose, enlist, encounter, embark*

epi—upon, at, over...*epicanthus, epicene, epicenter, episode, epicranium, epicycle, epidemic, epidermis, epitaph, epigraph, epilogue*

equi—equal...*equiangular, equilibrium, equidistant, equilateral, equinox, equity, equitable, equivalent, equivocal*

eu—good...*Eucharist, euthanasia, eugenics, eulogy, eupepsia, euphemism, euphonious, euphoria, eureka*

ex—out of, from, beyond...*express, exceed, exhaust, excel, excuse, exhale, excess, export, extract, extreme, expel, explain*

extra—outside, beyond...*extracurricular, extrajudicial, extraneous, extraordinary, extrapolate, extrasensory, extravagant, extraterrestrial*

MORE . . .

hetero—different...*heterochromatic, heterogeneous, heteromorphic, heterosexual, heterodox*

homo—same...*homochromatic, homogeneous, homogenize, homograph, homophone, homonym, homologous, homosexual*

hyper—over, above...*hyperactive, hypertension, hypersensitive, hypercritical, hyperglycemia, hyperbola, hyperbole*

hypo—under, beneath, below...*hypochondriac, hypocrisy, hypocrite, hypodermic, hypoglycemia, hypotension, hypotenuse, hypothesis*

im, in—in, not...*impossible, immigrate, impatient, import, immoral, incorrect, invisible, incomplete, inhale, insane, install*

inter—between, among, from one to another...*interpret, intercede, interrupt, intermission, interval, international, interstate, intervene, interact, intercept*

intra—within, inside...*intrastate, intramural, intravenous, intramuscular, intracity, intradermal, intramolecular, intracellular*

intro—into, inside...*introduce, introduction, introject, introspect, introspection, introvert, introversion*

iso—equal, alike...*isobar, isochromatic, isosceles, isocracy, isocyclic, isotope, isogenous, isomer, isometric, isomorphic, isotherm*

macro, maxi, mega—large, long...*maxim, maximum, megaphone, megalopolis, macron, macroscopic, macroeconomics,*

mal—bad, wrong...*maladjusted, maladroit, malady, malaise, malign, malice, malapropism, malaria, malefaction, malevolence, malfunction*

meta—changed, after, beyond, between...*metabolism, metazoa, metacenter, metachromatism, metagalaxy, metaphysical, metamorphosis, metaphor*

micro—small...*microphone, microfilm, microscope, microwave, microsecond, microfiche, microbe, micrometer, micron, microorganism*

mid—middle...*midland, midline, midnight, midpoint, midriff, midstream, midsummer, midway, midweek, midwife, midwinter*

mis—bad, wrong...*misbehave, misspell, misinform, misconduct, miscount, misfit, mishap, mislead, misfortune, misjudge, misinterpret*

MORE...

mono—one, single...*monorail, monoplane, monologue, monosyllabic, monolingual, monocle, monograph, monophobia, monopoly, monotone*

multi—many, much...*multilevel, multilingual, multimillionaire, multipurpose, multivitamins, multiplication, multitude, multimedia*

neo—new...*Neocene, neoclassic, neolithic, neologism, neon, neonatal, neophyte, neoplasm, neomycin*

neg, non—not...*negative, neglect, negligent, negotiate, nonfiction, nonsense, nonstop, noncompliance, nonconformity, none*

omni—all, everywhere...*omnibus, omnidirectional, omnific, omnipotence, omnipresent, omniscience, omniscient, omnivore*

out—greater, beyond, outer place...*outdo, outrun, outlive, outcast, outdated, outbid, outboard, outburst, outfield, outdoors, outside, outpost, outbound*

over—beyond, too much...*overall, overcome, overhead, overdrawn, oversleep, overrated, overseas, oversized, overstep, overdo, overdue*

para—beside, beyond, by, protect from, almost...*parable, parasite, parachute, paraphrase, paradise, paradox, paragon, paragraph, parallel, paralysis, paramedic, paranoid*

per—away, through, very...*perception, percolate, perdurable, perennial, perforate, perform, perfume, perfunctory, perfect*

peri—about, surrounding...*perigee, perimeter, perinatal, period, periodontal, periscope, peripatetic, peripheral, periphery*

poly—many, much...*polychrome, polydactyl, polygamy, polygraph, Polynesia, polyp, polyphonic, polyurethane, polygon*

post—after...*postpone, postscript, posterior, posthumous, posthypnotic, postgraduate, postpaid, postmortem, postwar, postdate*

pre—before...*preschool, prepaid, prepare, predict, precaution, preamble, prerecord, prescribe, preserve, presume, precook, prefix*

pro—before, for, onward...*promote, progress, provide, protect, prognosis, project, program, prologue, proceed, pronoun, protract, propose*

MORE . . .

pseudo—false...*pseudonym, pseudonymous, pseudoscience, pseudoclassic, pseudopod, pseudomorph, pseudopregnancy, pseudosalt*

re—back, again...*recall, renew, rebuild, retrace, repay, regain, rewrite, rejoin, reappear, rearrange, recall, return, react, recount*

retro—back, behind...*retroactive, retrofire, retroflex, retrograde, retrogress, retrorocket, retrospect, retrofit*

sub—under, below, secondary, next...*submarine, subject, submerge, subordinate, subterranean, subdue, subliminal, subdivision, submit, subtract, subway*

super—over, above, superior, more than...*supernatural, superhuman, superpower, superimpose, supersede, supersonic, supervisor, superintendent*

syl, sym, syn—together...*syllable, syllogism, symbiosis, symbol, symmetry, sympathy, symphony, symposium, synchronize, synthesize, synthetic*

tele—distant, over, from...*telephone, telegraph, television, telecommunication, telecast, telephoto, telepathy, telescope, telegram*

trans—across, over, through...*transatlantic, transcend, transcribe, transform, transfer, translate, transportation, transmit, transaction, transplant*

ultra—beyond...*ultraconservative, ultramarine, ultramicroscopic, ultrared, ultramodern, ultrasonic, ultrasound, ultraviolet, ultravirus*

un—not, the reverse of...*unable, undo, untie, unfair, unbeatable, unborn, uncertain, uncommon, uncover, uneasy, unexpected, unhappy, unleaded*

under—less than, below...*undercover, underground, underwear, underline, undergraduate, underpass, underage, underhand*

WORD STORIES

The most effective teachers make words interesting and exciting to students. They guide them through activities to help them develop their vocabularies and their understanding of words and how they are spelled.

Word "stories" are interesting to students. For example, knowing a word's origin often helps students remember the word better for meaning as well as spelling. Exploring words we've borrowed from other languages is exciting to students. From the French we have an abundant collection which includes a la carte (ordered as separate items on a menu), bouquet, unique, antique, ballet, cafe, and plateau. Compound words were in many instances once two words that were used so often together that they became one word. Students like collecting interesting words—palindromes (spelled the same forward as backward), onomatopoeia words (words that sound like what they mean—bang, buzz, quack).

Books can be a catalyst for developing an interest in words. Here are examples:

Dandelions Don't Bite: The Story of Words, Leone Adelson; Pantheon, 1972; Grades 3-5

A Book About the Origins of Everyday Words and Phrases, Jane Sarnoff; Scribner, 1981; Grades 5-8

What's That You Said? How Words Change, Ann E. Weiss; Harcourt, 1980; Grades 1-3

101 Words and How They Began, Arthur Steckler; Doubleday, 1979; Grades 2-4

Wordlore, David Hilliam; W & R Chambers, 1984; Grade 6 and above

Word Mysteries and Histories, Editors American Heritage Dictionary; Houghton, 1986; Grade 6 and above

The Guinness Book of Words, Martin Manser; Guinness, 1988; Grade 6 and above

Extraordinary Origins of Everyday Things, Charles Panati; Harper & Row, 1987; Grade 6 and above

Traffic: A Book of Opposites, Betsy Maestro; Crown, 1991; Grades 1-3

Hey, Hay!: A Wagonful of Funny Homonym Riddles, Marvin Terban; Clarion, 1991; Grades 4-8

Herds of Words, Patricia MacCarthy; Dial, 1991; Grades 1-3

Seeing, Saying, Doing, Playing: A Big Book of Action Words, Taro Gomi; Chronicle, 1991; Grades 1-3

Up, Up and Away: A Book About Adverbs, Ruth Heller; Grosset, 1991; Grades 1-3

Sparkle and Spin: A Book About Words, Ann and Paul Rand; Abrams, 1991; Grades 1-3

All About Overnight: A Book of Compound Words, Betsy Maestro; Clarion, 1992; Grades 1-3

MORE...

EPONYMS !

Students particularly like <u>eponyms</u>, or words that were <u>named for a person or a place</u>. Introduce students to eponyms with *Guppies in Tuxedos: Funny Eponyms* (Marvin Terban; Clarion, 1988). Here are examples of eponyms...

afghan—<u>Afghanistan's</u> wool coverlets became known as afghans, though now any coverlet is called an afghan.

America—The Italian, <u>Amerigo Vespucci</u> worked for a company that outfitted ships for Columbus and others. He wrote stories about his own voyages. A mapmaker believed that Amerigo had discovered the New World, so he called it America on his maps in Amerigo's honor. Spain called the New World Columbia after Columbus, but this name never became popular.

ampere—<u>Andre-Marie Ampere</u> was a French scientist. He discovered a way of measuring the strength of an electric current. The measurement is called an ampere, or amp.

atlas—<u>Atlas</u> was the giant of strength in Greek myths. Many geography and map books pictured on their cover Atlas holding a globe on his back. Soon the book was called an atlas.

beef stroganoff—Count <u>Paul Stroganoff</u> was a Russian diplomat. He liked this fancy beef dinner.

beef wellington—The <u>Duke of Wellington</u> was a British Prime Minister and military hero. This fancy beef dinner was named for him.

bikini—The US tested atom bombs on the island <u>Bikini Atoll</u>. When the daring swimsuit was introduced at a Paris fashion show, it made a "hit like the atom bomb." So it was referred to as the bikini.

bloomers—Mrs. <u>Amelia Bloomer</u> was the American lady who popularized the baggy pants gathered at the ankle worn under a skirt.

bobby—A police officer in England is called a "bobby." The name came from the well-liked <u>Sir Robert Peel</u> who reorganized the London police.

bologna—The northern Italian city <u>Bologna</u> became famous for its smoked sausage. The sausage was called bologna, or baloney.

bowie knife—<u>James Bowie</u> fought in pioneer days for Texas freedom. He used a long single-edged hunting knife.

boycott—Captain <u>Charles Boycott</u> was an Irish landlord who refused to lower rents, so the storekeepers refused to sell to him.

braille—<u>Louis Braille</u> was blind. A system of raised dots and dashes used in the French military gave him the idea of inventing a system of raised dots for alphabet letters to use to communicate among the blind.

bunsen burner—This flame used in some science experiments was invented by Professor <u>Robert Bunsen</u>, a German chemist.

canary—The <u>Canary Islands</u> were the first place canaries were found.

MORE . . .

candy—The young French <u>Prince of Conde</u> disliked healthy foods. The palace chef disguised these foods with a sugar coating to get the prince to eat them. As a result, sugary food became known as candy.

canter—This easy galloping pace was first called the <u>Canterbury</u> gallop. It is the pace the English often chose to ride their horses to Canterbury to see the shrine of St. Thomas a Becket.

cardigan—James Thomas Brudenell, the seventh <u>Earl of Cardigan</u>, first wore a sweater that buttoned down the front. This kind of sweater became known as a cardigan.

Celsius—<u>Anders Celsius</u>, a Swedish astronomer, invented the centigrade temperature scale on which water freezes at 0 degrees.

cereal—<u>Ceres</u> was the Roman goddess of grain, harvests, fruit, and farming.

chauvinist—Originally, chauvinists were people very loyal to their country and its leaders. The word came from <u>Nicholas Chauvin</u> who had a fanatical devotion to Napoleon.

cheddar cheese—<u>Cheddar</u>, a village in England, was the first place people ate this hard, smooth cheese.

decibel—<u>Alexander Graham Bell</u> invented the telephone and many other electronic devices. Decibels were named for him which measure the loudness of sounds.

derrick—<u>Thomas Derrick</u> was an English hangman. His name became known for death by hanging and the apparatus, like a crane, used for the hanging. Now some cranes for lifting and moving heavy objects are called derricks.

derringer—<u>Henry Deringer</u> was a Philadelphia gun-maker who made this little pistol often seen in Old West movies. Over the years, an "r" was added to the name of the gun.

diesel—<u>Rudolf Diesel</u> was the German engineer who invented the diesel engine. It uses fuel oil instead of gasoline.

duffel bag, duffel coat—The town of <u>Duffel</u> near Antwerp in Belgium was the first place duffel cloth was made. It is thick, coarse cloth used in making bags and coats.

dunce—<u>John Duns Scotus</u>, a Scottish theologian and writer, was mocked because of his backward ideas. A "slow learner" soon began to be called a duns, or dunce.

Fahrenheit—<u>Gabriel Fahrenheit</u>, a German physicist, invented the temperature scale on which water freezes at 32 degrees.

Ferris wheel—<u>George Washington Ferris</u>, an engineer, created the first Ferris wheel for the 1893 Chicago World's Fair.

frisbee—The original frisbees were pie pans from the Frisbie Pie Company started by <u>William R. Frisbie</u> in Bridgeport, Connecticut. It was the nearby Yale students who initiated the sport.

galvanize—<u>Luigi Galvani</u> was the Italian scientist who produced an electrical current that made a dead frog's legs move. Many electrical processes and devices bear his name. However, the word we think of most often is "galvanized," or activated, like the frog's legs.

graham crackers and graham flour—<u>Rev. Sylvester Graham</u> was a US diet reformer who advocated eating healthy foods, including whole wheat flour instead of white flour.

MORE . . .

guillotine—Dr. <u>Joseph Guillotine</u> supported the use of the guillotine for killing people during the French Revolution.

guppy—<u>R. J. Lechmere Guppy</u> discovered this little tropical fish in Trinidad, which now is often in home aquariums.

guy—<u>Guy Fawkes</u> Day in England is November 5 and recognizes the capture of this man before he could destroy the Parliament building and King James I. Children make funny- looking dummies of Guy out of rags for the occasion. In England a "guy" is a funny-looking man. In America it is slang for any fellow.

hoodlum—A San Francisco writer wrote about a crook named <u>Muldoon</u>, but he was afraid to use his real name. Instead he used the name spelled backwards, Noodlum. A printer's mistake changed the name to Hoodlum. Soon all crooks were called hoodlums, or just hoods.

jeans—The city of Genoa is spelled <u>Genes</u> in French. The strong material out of which jeans are made came from this city. It was the American Levi Strauss who made this material into "levis," or jeans.

leotard—<u>Jules Leotard</u> created skin-tight clothing to wear during his trapeze act in the French circus. Similar clothing today is called a leotard.

levis—<u>Levi Strauss</u> made heavy work pants for the California Gold Rush miners. They became known as levis after Mr. Strauss' first name.

marathon—In 490 B.C. a messenger ran 26 miles from <u>Marathon</u>, a plain in eastern Greece, to Athens to tell about the winning of an important battle. Today the 26-mile endurance races are called marathons.

maverick—Texan <u>Sam Maverick</u> didn't brand his cattle. The unbranded cattle became known as mavericks. Now any person acting independently of the crowd may be called a maverick.

mesmerize—<u>F. A. Mesmer</u> was an Austrian doctor who often hypnotized his patients. Soon the two words were synonyms.

Morse code—<u>Samuel Morse</u> devised a coded system of short and long beeps or flashes of light to communicate. The best known pattern is the distress signal SOS (...---...).

napoleons—These pastry treats were first made by <u>Neapolitans</u>, the people of Naples, Italy. They called them napolitains, but that was too hard for some people to say. People started calling them napoleons.

OK—<u>Martin Van Buren</u> was often called Old Kinderhook after his New York hometown, Kinderhook. It was shortened to OK. When he ran for reelection to the presidency, his signs said "Vote Right. Vote OK." The OK came to mean all right, fine, or terrific.

oldsmobile—<u>Ransom E. Olds</u> made the oldsmobile in his Olds Motor Works. It was the first commercially successful car in America.

panic—The mythical Greek god <u>Pan</u> used to scare travelers out of their wits. Now panic means "a strong fear among people that causes them to act out of control."

pants—<u>Pantaloons</u> was an Old Italian comedy character. He always wore the same red trousers. Soon all trousers were called pantaloons. Then that was shortened to pants.

MORE . . .

pasteurized—<u>Louis Pasteur</u>, a French scientist, discovered a method of ridding germs from milk. Milk that has undergone this process is said to have been pasteurized.

pickles—Dutchman <u>Willem Beukelz</u> (said BOY-kells) was the first person to "pickle" food to preserve it before the invention of refrigerators. English people called pickled cucumbers "pickles," a mispronunciation of Beukelz.

peach Melba—<u>Helen "Melba" Mitchell</u>, an Australian opera singer, was so admired by a French chef that he named a peach and ice cream dessert in her honor.

pullman—<u>George Pullman</u> spent all his money building one luxury railroad car. But the railroads said it was too big. Later, a big car was needed for President Lincoln's funeral train. They used Pullman's. After that, many travelers wanted the bigger cars, or pullmans.

rugby—<u>Rugby</u> is the English town in which the football-like game of rugby was first played.

sandwich—The <u>Earl of Sandwich</u> did not want to leave his gambling table to eat. He had his servant bring him "meat between two pieces of bread," now our word for sandwich.

saxophone—<u>Antoine Sax</u> from Belgium invented and made the first saxophones.

scrooge—<u>Ebenezer Scrooge</u>, the grumpy miser in the book *A Christmas Carol*, was the origin of this word that means the kind of person he was.

sideburns—<u>US General Ambrose Everett Burnside</u> wore whiskers down the side of his face. People began calling them in his honor, sideburns.

silhouette—<u>Etienne de Silhouette</u> was a French politician who raised taxes. To oppose the increases, his side-view face was drawn on black placards.

tantalize—An old Greek story told about <u>King Tantalus</u> who gave away the god's secrets. For punishment, the gods made him stand in neck-deep water with wonderful food just out of his reach. Because of the story, when we tease people with something they cannot have, we "tantalize" them.

teddy bear—<u>Theodore Roosevelt</u> (sometimes called Teddy) once saved the life of a little brown bear cub. After that, stuffed bear toys were often called "teddy bears."

tuxedo—At a formal party at the fancy <u>Tuxedo Park Country Club</u> in New York, a man came dressed in a new-style suit fashioned after a suit the Prince of Wales wore. First they became known as Tuxedo Park suits, then just tuxedos, and now often just a "tux."

vandal—In A.D. 455 a tribe roamed Europe robbing and setting fires. They were the Vandals. Today anyone who maliciously destroys property is a vandal and vandalizes.

volt—Alessandro Volta, an Italian physicist, contributed to our understanding of electrical force. Also, eponyms are the electrical terms "amps or amperes" (Andre-Marie Ampere), "ohms" (George Ohm), and "watts" (James Watt).

 ...also many eponyms are found among the following: names of cars (Ford), flowers (dahlia), trees (sequoia), foods (hamburger), breeds of animals (labrador dog), days of the week (Sunday), months (July), states (Washington), and cities (Columbus).

Shortcut words include <u>contractions</u>, <u>clipped words</u>, and <u>abbreviations</u>.

These are among <u>the most commonly used contractions</u>:

am:	I'm
are:	you're, we're, they're
is, has:	he's, she's, it's, what's, that's, who's, there's, here's
us:	let's
had, would:	I'd, you'd, he'd, she'd, we'd, they'd
have:	I've, you've, we've, they've
not:	can't, don't, isn't, won't, shouldn't, couldn't, wouldn't, aren't, doesn't, wasn't, weren't, hasn't, haven't, hadn't, mustn't, didn't
will:	I'll, you'll, she'll, he'll, it'll, we'll, they'll

Here are <u>examples of several words we often clip or shorten</u>. Sometimes the students are familiar only with the clipped version and are unaware that the words have a longer form.

ad = advertisement	limo = limousine
auto = automobile	lube = lubricate
bike = bicycle	lunch = luncheon
burger = hamburger	mart = market
bus = omnibus	math = mathematics
cab = cabriolet	mike = microphone
cent = centum	mend = amend
champ = champion	memo = memorandum
chemist = alchemist	movie = moving picture
clerk = cleric	mum = chrysanthemum
coed = coeducational	pants = pantaloons
con = convict	pen = penitentiary
cop = copper	phone = telephone
cuke = cucumber	plane = airplane
curio = curiosity	prof = professor
doc = doctor	ref = referee
dorm = dormitory	scram = scramble
drape = drapery	sis = sister
exam = examination	sub = submarine
flu = influenza	taxi = taxicab
fridge = refrigerator	teen = teenager
fries = french fries	tie = necktie
gas = gasoline	tux = tuxedo
grad = graduate	van = caravan
gym = gymnasium	vet - veteran, veterinarian
lab = laboratory	zoo = zoological garden

MORE . . .

<u>Abbreviations are another example of shortcut words.</u> These are among the most commonly used abbreviations:

adjective	adj.	manager	mgr.
adverb	adv.	medium	med.
and others	etc.	meter	m
assistant	asst.	midnight-noon hours	a.m./A.M
avenue	ave.	miles per hour	mph
building	bldg.	milliliter	mL
capital	cap.	minute	min
centimeter	cm	miscellaneous	misc.
chapter	chap.	month	mo
company	co.	noon-midnight hours	p.m./P.M.
conjunction	conj.	number	no.
corporation	corp.	ounce	oz
department	dept.	package	pkg.
division	div.	page	p./pg.
dozen	doz	pages	pp.
each	ea.	paid	pd
example	ex.	pint	pt
foot or feet	ft	plural	pl.
gallon	gal	population	pop.
government	gvt.	pound	lb
gram	g	president	pres.
hospital	hosp.	principal	prin
hour	hr.	pronoun	pron.
illustration	illus.	quart	qt
inch	in.	seconds	sec
kilogram	kg	singular	sing
kilometer	km	square	sq
kilometers per hour	kph	street	st.
latitude	lat.	subject	subj.
liter	L	telephone	tel.
longitude	long.	weight	wt.
		year	yr

January	Jan.	Monday	Mon.
February	Feb.	Tuesday	Tues.
March	Mar.	Wednesday	Wed.
April	Apr.	Thursday	Thurs.
August	Aug.	Friday	Fri.
September	Sept.	Saturday	Sat.
October	Oct.	Sunday	Sun.
November	Nov.		
December	Dec.		

MORE . . .

Alabama	AL	Montana	MT
Alaska	AK	Nebraska	NE
Arizona	AZ	Nevada	NV
Arkansas	AR	New Hampshire	NH
California	CA	New Jersey	NJ
Colorado	CO	New Mexico	NM
Connecticut	CT	New York	NY
Delaware	DE	North Carolina	NC
Florida	FL	North Dakota	ND
Georgia	GA	Ohio	OH
Hawaii	HI	Oklahoma	OK
Idaho	ID	Oregon	OR
Illinois	IL	Pennsylvania	PA
Indiana	IN	Rhode Island	RI
Iowa	IA	South Carolina	SC
Kansas	KS	South Dakota	SD
Kentucky	KY	Tennessee	TN
Louisiana	LA	Texas	TX
Maine	ME	Utah	UT
Maryland	MD	Vermont	VT
Massachusetts	MA	Virginia	VA
Michigan	MI	Washington	WA
Minnesota	MN	West Virginia	WV
Mississippi	MS	Wisconsin	WI
Missouri	MO	Wyoming	WY

Alberta	AB
British Columbia	BC
Manitoba	MB
New Brunswick	NB
Newfoundland	NF
Northwest Territories	NT
Nova Scotia	NS
Ontario	ON
Prince Edward Island	PE
Quebec	PQ
Saskatchewan	SK
Yukon Territories	YT

MORE...

<u>Blended words are shortcut words</u>. They are two words blended together that take on a new meaning...a meaning that combines the meanings of its two parts. Sometimes these words are called portmanteaus.

Here are examples...

                  autobus...automobile + bus
                  bit...binary + digit
                  blotch...blot + botch
                  brunch...breakfast + lunch
                  chortle...chuckle + snort
                  clump...chunk + lump
                  conman...confidence + man
                  farewell...fare + thee + well
                  flare...flame + glare
                  flurry...flutter + hurry
                  fortnight...fourteen + nights
                  glimmer...gleam + shimmer
                  goodbye...God + be with + you
                  hifi...high + fidelity
                  infomercial...information + commercial
                  moped...motor + pedal
                  motel...motor + hotel
                  motorcade...motor + cavalcade
                  o'clock...of + the + clock
                  skylab...sky + laboratory
                  slosh...slop + slush
                  smash...smack + mash
                  smog...smoke + fog
                  sparsity...sparse + scarcity
                  splatter...splash + spatter
                  squiggle...squirm + wiggle
                  telethon...television + marathon
                  twirl...twist + whirl

Dictation can play an important role in spelling and language acquisition. Consider these options for <u>READY-MADE DICTATION</u> activities for your curriculum:

Use the often-included dictation in the activities of SPELLING SOURCEBOOKS 2, 3, and 4. These sentences or paragraphs are all vocabulary controlled and open-ended. After the dictation, students finish the sentences for the paragraph.

NEW! Use the Dictation Review in the new <u>SPELLING SOURCEBOOK REVIEWS</u> (see <u>Rebecca Sitton's Materials</u> section in this handbook). Each Dictation Review is a vocabulary-controlled sentence dictation activity focusing on a set of five Core Words sequentially 1-1200. It is accompanied by a Blackline Master Cloze Story focusing on the same five Core Words and previously-introduced words. The REVIEWS provide ongoing reinforcement with the most challenging words for their ultimate mastery in writing. They also provide a measure for assessing students' progress toward mastery of the words.

Teachers can allow students to use spelling references for dictation, or they can disallow the use of a reference, such as the Priority Word list. Teachers may dictate the sentences...then provide the sentences (blackline master, chalkboard, etc.) so that students proofread their word correcting errors. Or teachers can correct the sentences. Some teachers make the sentences available for students to study ahead of time, while other do not. There are many formats that work well. Multiple ideas are included for dictation in the teaching notes of the REVIEWS.

Departmentalized teachers, especially in a junior high/middle school, need options for spelling instruction that specifically meet their time constraints and the number of students they teach. Following are suggestions:

First, it should be noted that if the Core Words were taken from the list of 1200 in SPELLING SOURCEBOOK 1, the words from 1000-1200 were edited for instructional appropriateness. Phonetically uncomplicated words with few letters were omitted, including only instructional relevant words at the upper grades. The ready-made activities to teach and expand these Core Words in SPELLING SOURCEBOOK 4 are motivational and relevant to upper grade instruction.

Yet, working with the Core Words and the Springboard Activities won't provide the most mileage for time-limited spelling instruction. So, when the Core Words are divided by grade levels, fewer total words could be assigned to the junior high/middle school teachers. Or, these teachers should not feel guilty hand-picking words and activities they wish to use among those Core Words assigned to their grades.

MORE . . .

To get the most spelling growth in writing in the least amount of time, junior high/middle school teachers should emphasize the Priority Words. Students could be given a set of Priority Words (perhaps the top 200) with the expectation that these words are unacceptable to misspell in any everyday writing assignment (writing-process papers remain at 100% accuracy). The requirement is to spell and use the Priority Words accurately in all everyday writing, for any teacher, in any subject. Additional writing-relevant words could be added, either permanently or for topical writing pieces.

Random writing samples (perhaps 3-5) can be selected during each grading period from each student to determine how well the expectation is being met. Then, spelling grades should be based on this information. Any student misspelling or misusing any of the Priority Words on the samples selected for assessment should have a reduced grade for spelling. It works best to have spelling as a separate grade on the report card. This clearly establishes spelling as an important skill, but does not penalize students' other grades (science, social studies, writing) if their spelling is below standards.

It is <u>unnecessary to check a whole paper</u> for Priority Words. Brackets in the paper's margin can indicate the parts selected for Priority Word assessment. Papers should be checked just often enough to communicate: "The teacher is looking...and cares."

To afford students maximum practice in learning to be accountable for their Priority Words, students must be made aware that a writing sample can come from any one of their teachers. Spelling growth will be minimal if it is practiced solely within the time frame of writing class. The language arts/English teacher should occasionally take a writing sample for just a few students from the content teachers to convey the message that spelling counts in all subjects. If necessary, a copy of the content paper can be made so that the original paper can stay with the content teacher.

STUDENTS WITH SPECIAL NEEDS...

Students with special spelling challenges can learn to spell. First, a teacher must decide if the student can remain in the Core Word part of the program. If the student cannot read the Core Words, the words are inappropriate for spelling. However, the student could take part in the Preview-Review. (See blackline example, page 124, for a modified method for these students to take the Preview-Review. This method also works well for some first graders who aren't ready to begin spelling when the others begin and for ESL/bilingual students learning English.)

It's important for these students to take part in the integrated-language Springboard Activities with the class that help all students make critical language connections. Also, these students need a **realistic** Priority Word list, perhaps the first ten high-use words. They must spell these ten words correctly in **all their writing**. Later, three more words can be added making the students responsible for thirteen words, then fifteen, and so on. This step-by-step growth is not intimidating to these students. The system sets a reasonable goal and builds on it over time. As more words are added in sequence, misspellings may begin to occur among some of the first words on the list. Then, spelling instruction can focus on the **recurring** problem words, relying heavily on visual skill-building activities.

For more information see pages 113-115. (Also see Articles 7 and 13 of SPELLING SOURCEBOOK 1 for more ideas to assist students with special spelling needs.) The SPELLING SOURCEBOOK Reviews can be modified for successful use with students challenged by spelling. See the front matter in the Reviews for teaching notes that offer suggestions for modification.

THE CAPABLE SPELLER

How can the most capable speller be challenged? First, who is a **capable speller**? A capable speller spells consistently well in **writing**.

Following are suggestions for challenging capable spellers.

1. Assign the more sophisticated Springboard Activities to these students, many of which could be called "projects." There are ready-made Springboard Activities for every Core Word in SPELLING SOURCEBOOKS 2, 3, and 4 (see <u>Rebecca Sitton's Materials</u> section). Have students present their completed projects to the class.

2. Give these students more opportunities to write.

3. Increase their number of Priority Words.

4. Increase their number of topical reference words designated for spelling accuracy beyond the list for which the class is responsible.

5. Engage the students in an Individualized List of additional words (see pages 54-56). Words can be added by the students, their parents, and teachers.

6. Have these students create spelling games and activities for other students to complete, such as cloze-dictation activities.

7. Make these students the Class Editors, occasionally helping the teacher proofread papers for spelling.

8. Have high expectations for spelling on the SPELLING SOURCEBOOK Reviews—the dictations and cloze activities can be highly challenging.

OFTEN-CONFUSED WORDS

There are many sets of English words that sound somewhat alike and/or look somewhat alike, but are different words with different meanings and uses. Some of these words are represented on the high-frequency list, while others are used less frequently. However, all are frequently used incorrectly. Many of these words may also be confused with homophones and homographs.

 Here are some examples...

acme/acne
adjoin/adjourn
accede/exceed/a seed
access/assess/excess
a cost/accost
adapt/adept/adopt
advice/advise
a field/afield
a head/ahead
a long/along
allude/elude
amoral/moral/morale/immoral/immortal
a part/apart
a piece/a peace/apiece
a portion/apportion
a ray/array
a sign/assign
a test/attest
a tract/attract
aural/oral
a vow/avow
a way/away
all ready/already
allusion/delusion/illusion
anecdote/antidote
annual/annul
appraise/apprise
assure/ensure/insure
bibliography/biography
casual/causal
census/consensus/senses
choral/chorale/coral/corral
coma/comma
comprehensible/comprehensive
conscience/conscious/conscientious
continual/continuous
cooperation/corporation/corroboration
credible/creditable/credulous
dairy/diary
decent/descent/dissent

abettor/a better/a bettor
a cent/a scent/ascent/assent
accent/ascent/assent
a cross/across
a cyst/assist
a drift/adrift
adverse/averse/a verse
a foot/afoot
a lone/a loan/alone
a lot/allot
a maze/amaze
a parent/apparent
a peal/a peel/appeal
a point/appoint
a rest/arrest
are/our
a tack/attack
a tire/attire
a tune/attune
a void/avoid
a ward/award
all right/alright (not a word)
all together/altogether
all ways/always
angel/angle
any one/anyone
area/aria
biannual/biennial
breadth/breath/breathe
cease/seize
choose/chose
collision/collusion
command/commend
confidant/confident
contagious/contiguous
core/corps/corpse
costume/custom
crumble/crumple
deceased/diseased
deference/difference

MORE....

deposition/disposition
deprecate/depreciate
desolate/dissolute
device/devise
disburse/disperse
disinterested/uninterested
elapse/lapse/relapse
eligible/illegible
emerge/immerge
emigrate/immigrate
emanate/eminent/imminent/immanent
enviable/envious
every body/everybody
every one/everyone
expect/suspect
extant/extent
facet/faucet
facility/felicity
finale/finally/finely
flammable/inflammable
fury/furry
human/humane
in to/into
imply/infer
indigenous/indigent/indignant
jealous/zealous
least/less/lest
lightening/lightning
magnate/magnet
medal/meddle/metal
mumble/murmur/mutter
patrol/petrol
perfect/prefect
perquisite/prerequisite
personal/personnel
peruse/pursue
precede/proceed
pretend/portend
receipt/recipe
respectable/respectful/respective
revolve/rotate
some time(s)/sometime(s)
status/stature/statute
thorough/though/through
unit/unite
veracious/voracious
weather/whether
your/you're

depraved/deprived
desert/dessert
detract/distract
disapprove/disprove
discomfit/discomfort
dispense/disperse/distribute
elicit/illicit
elusive/illusive
emigrant/immigrant
empire/umpire
envelop/envelope
erasable/irascible
every day/everyday
expand/expend
explicit/implicit
extort/extract
facilitate/felicitate
farther/further
fiscal/physical
formally/formerly
genius/genus
hypercritical/hypocritical
imitate/intimate/intimidate
incredible/incredulous
ingenious/ingenuous
later/latter
liable/libel
loose/lose
may be/maybe
morality/mortality
no body/nobody
peaceable/peaceful
perpetrate/perpetuate
persecute/prosecute
perseverance/persistence
picture/pitcher
preposition/proposition
quiet/quit/quite
recent/resent
restive/restless
secede/succeed
suppose/supposed
than/then
through out/throughout
use/used
wear/where
were/we're

ABC Order

Prepare for the game by writing review spelling words on word cards. Place three word cards on each student's desk. Ask students to alphabetize their cards. As soon as students complete the task, quickly check their work. If the words are alphabetized correctly, give them another word card to alphabetize into the set. At any point in the game, if a student's words are not in correct ABC order, show the student the correct order, and replace the word cards with three new cards.

The object of the game is to get as many cards as possible. This depends upon speed as well as accuracy. As a follow-up activity, ask students to write their list of alphabetized words. Winners can post their lists on the bulletin board. ABC Order can be played in cooperative learning groups, too. Competition between groups is motivational.

All-Play Spelling Bee

Prepare for the game by writing review spelling words on word cards, each with a short context sentence confirming the meaning of the word. Divide the players into two teams of equal spelling ability. Give each team an equal number of word cards (about twice as many cards as players).

The first player on the starting team selects a word card, calls out the word, and reads it in the context sentence. The first player on the opposite team goes to the chalkboard and writes the word. Using the corrected-test procedure, the players check the spelling. If the word is correctly spelled, the word card is eliminated from the game. If the word is misspelled, it is written correctly, erased, and the word card is returned to the pile.

Players are never eliminated from the game, only word cards. The first team to eliminate the opposite team's word cards wins!

They're fine! However, academic "sports", like the athletic sports teams, must practice after school... not during class time. Create academic and athletic stars!

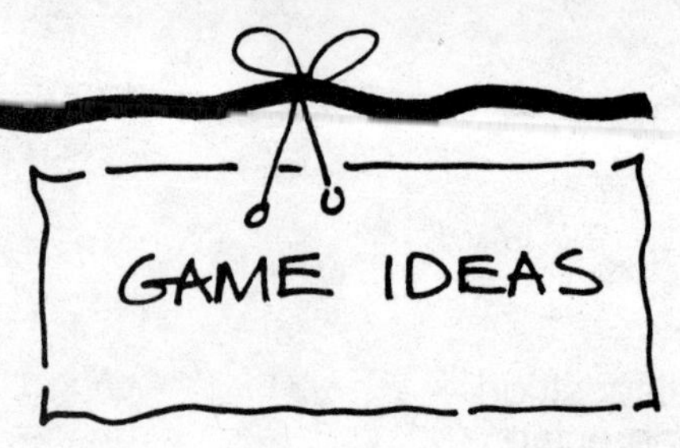

MORE...

Mr. Pickyfood

Prepare for the game by writing on the chalkboard the headings, LIKES and DOESN'T LIKE. Introduce the class to Mr. Pickyfood, a man who only eats what he likes. In the LIKES column, write peas, popcorn, and pumpkin pie. In the DOESN'T LIKE column, write jam, beans, and french fries. Go around the room asking students to suggest a food to see if it is one Mr. Pickyfood likes to eat. If the food begins with the letter "p," add it to the LIKES column. All other suggestions go in the DOESN'T LIKE list. The object of the game is to discover the reason for Mr. Pickyfood's pickiness (he only likes foods that begin with the letter "p"). Other foods to Mr. Pickyfood's liking might include pizza, potatoes, peanut butter, peaches, pasta, pot roast, pineapple, pepper, and pickles.

Mr. Pickyfood can be played using various reasons for his pickiness, such as foods with the long "e" sound, double letters, or five letters. Mr. Pickyfood has some picky cousins that make for entertaining word games, too. They are Miss Pickywear (clothes), Mrs. Pickypet (animals), and Mr. Pickypack (travel items). Can you think of others?

LIKES	DOESN'T LIKE
peas	lettuce
popcorn	cheese
peaches	beans
pizza	eggs
pasta	

Bingo

Prepare for the game by showing students how to fold a piece of writing paper into 16 boxes (four folds). Ask students to select spelling words from a list of about 20 words to write in the boxes of their paper. Words can be used only once in the boxes. Some words will be left over.

Decide which row or column will be Bingo.

Provide each student with a colored pencil.

The teacher begins the game by calling out a spelling word, using the word in a short sentence, and spelling and writing the word on the chalkboard (a student volunteer could spell and write the word). If students have the word in a box on their Bingo paper, they trace over the word with their colored pencil as the teacher spells it. If they do not, they turn the paper over and write the word on the back as the teacher spells it.

The first student to get Bingo wins, but play can continue until all words have been used.

MORE...

All in the Family

Prepare for the game by dividing students into cooperative learning groups. Each group will need paper and pencil.

The teacher begins the game by calling out a spelling word. The first player in each group writes the word. The paper and pencil is passed to the next member of the group and a derivative of the word is written. Each successive player writes a derivative until the group can think of no more, or until time is up (about three minutes). One point is awarded for the correct spelling of the base word and each of the derivatives. The group with the most points at the end of the game wins! Or the whole class wins a "prize" when the point total for all groups combined reaches a certain number.

Connect the Dots

Prepare for the game by providing each pair of students with a game sheet. The players will need paper, pencil, and their spelling books or a source for spelling words to be used in the game.

The first player selects a spelling word, pronounces it, and uses it in a short context sentence to confirm its meaning. The other player writes the word. Using the corrected-test procedure, the players check the spelling of the word. If the word is correctly spelled, that player may connect two dots on the game sheet. Roles then reverse and play continues.

The object of the game is to draw the last line to form a square on the game sheet and earn the number of points in the square. The player forming a square writes his/her name in the square. The player with the most points at the end of the game wins!

Connect the Dots can also be played by teams using a game board drawn on the chalkboard.

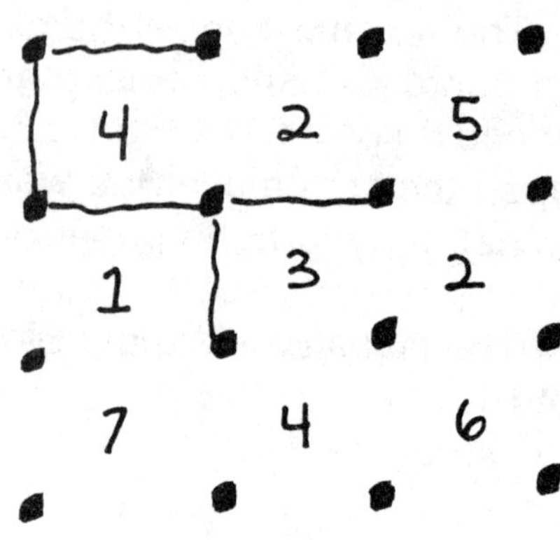

Prepare for the game by providing each student with a game sheet with letters or letter groups written in the squares. Students will need a pencil and paper to play. The object of the game is to list as many words as possible using the letters in the boxes. Words can be made by using letters in adjacent boxes only. Any letter can be doubled.

The game can be played individually with each player receiving a different game sheet, or with each player using the same game sheet. Spelling Squares can also be played in cooperative learning groups or as a brainstorming game for the whole class.

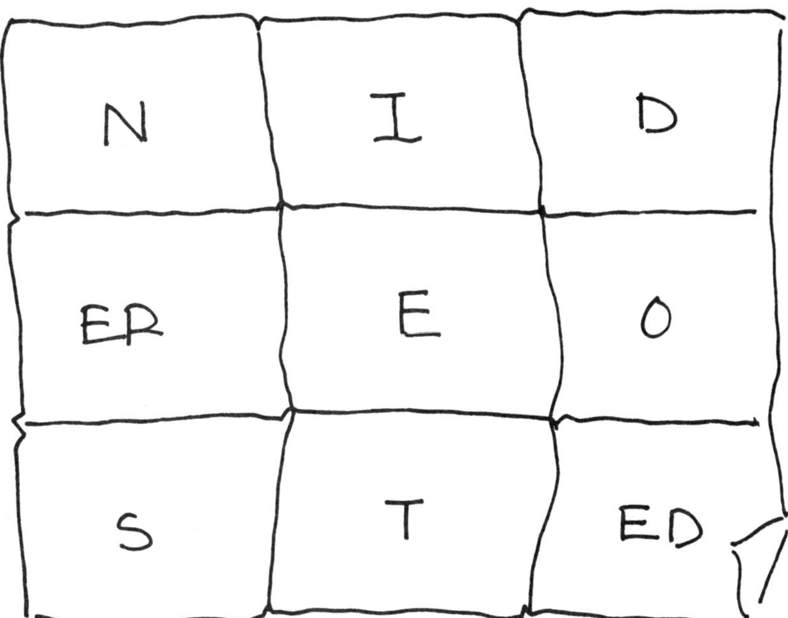

Spelling Baseball

Prepare for the game by arranging the classroom to accommodate a baseball diamond—three bases and home plate. Write review spelling words on word cards, each with a short context sentence confirming the meaning of the word. Divide the players into two teams. Determine how many innings there will be in the game.

The first team "at bat" sends their first player to bat. The first player on the opposite team "pitches" a word from the set of cards to the batter. The batter writes the word on the chalkboard.   Then the word is checked using the self-corrected test procedure. If the word is correct, the batter advances to first base and the second batter continues the game with the second player on the opposite team assuming the role of pitcher.

If a batter misses a word, it is an "out." Three outs and the opposite team is at bat. Points are scored by players crossing home plate—they advance one base for each word spelled correctly by a batter.

Play continues through the number of innings the class decides to play.

MORE . . .

Race Track Spelling

Prepare for the game by creating a "race track" on a large bulletin board. The race track consists of four long strips of construction paper of equal length (each a separate track) with about 15 spaces marked on each track. Divide the class into four teams. Ask each team to make a small race car of construction paper and name it. Pin each race car to one of the four tracks.

Play begins by asking one team member from each team to spell the same word. This can be done on paper, individual slate boards, or on the class chalkboard. If the class chalkboard is used, arrange the players so that they cannot see what one another has written.

Each player that spells the word correctly may advance the team race car one space. Play continues with team members spelling words until one race car crosses the finish line. That team is the winner.

Variations of the game include "Climb the Ladder" in which team members compete to climb each step of a ladder, "Go to the Moon" in which a moon is the destination that spaceships are trying to reach along a vertical course, or "Surfrider" that uses wave peaks as spaces to advance toward shore.

Spelling Boxes

Prepare for the game by making a matrix. Make copies of the matrix to use for future Spelling Boxes games. Using one of the matrix copies, fill in one word in each row. That word is the key word for the row. Each column must contain the same form of the word.

Students complete the empty boxes. They may use a dictionary for help if necessary.

Some boxes can be starred. These boxes indicate words that must be used in a sentence on a separate sheet of paper.

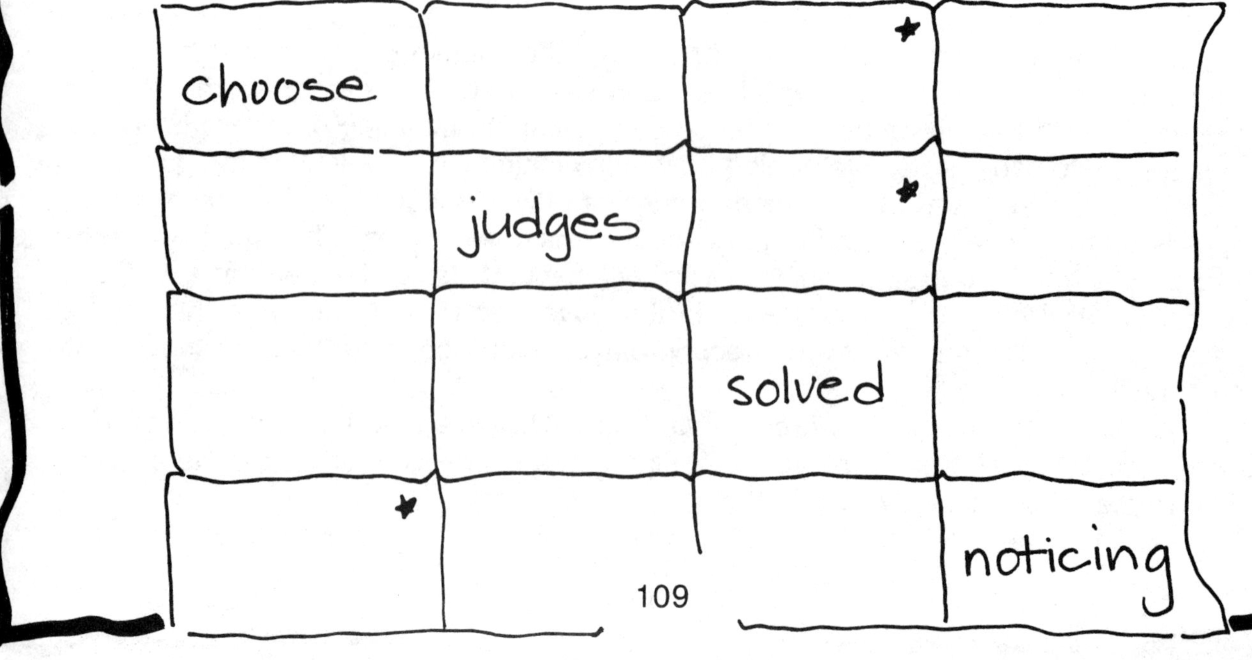

Prefix/Suffix Boxes

Prepare for the game by making a box divided into nine equal boxes. Make copies of this box to use for future Prefix/Suffix Boxes games. For Prefix Boxes, label each row with a different prefix. Label each column with an ending letter of a word. The students fill in the boxes using a word with the appropriate prefix and ending with the appropriate letter. For Suffix Boxes, label each row with a beginning letter for a word. Label each column with a suffix. The students fill in the boxes using a word with the appropriate beginning letter and ending with the appropriate suffix.

Have students share their games to make a cumulative list of correct responses for each box.

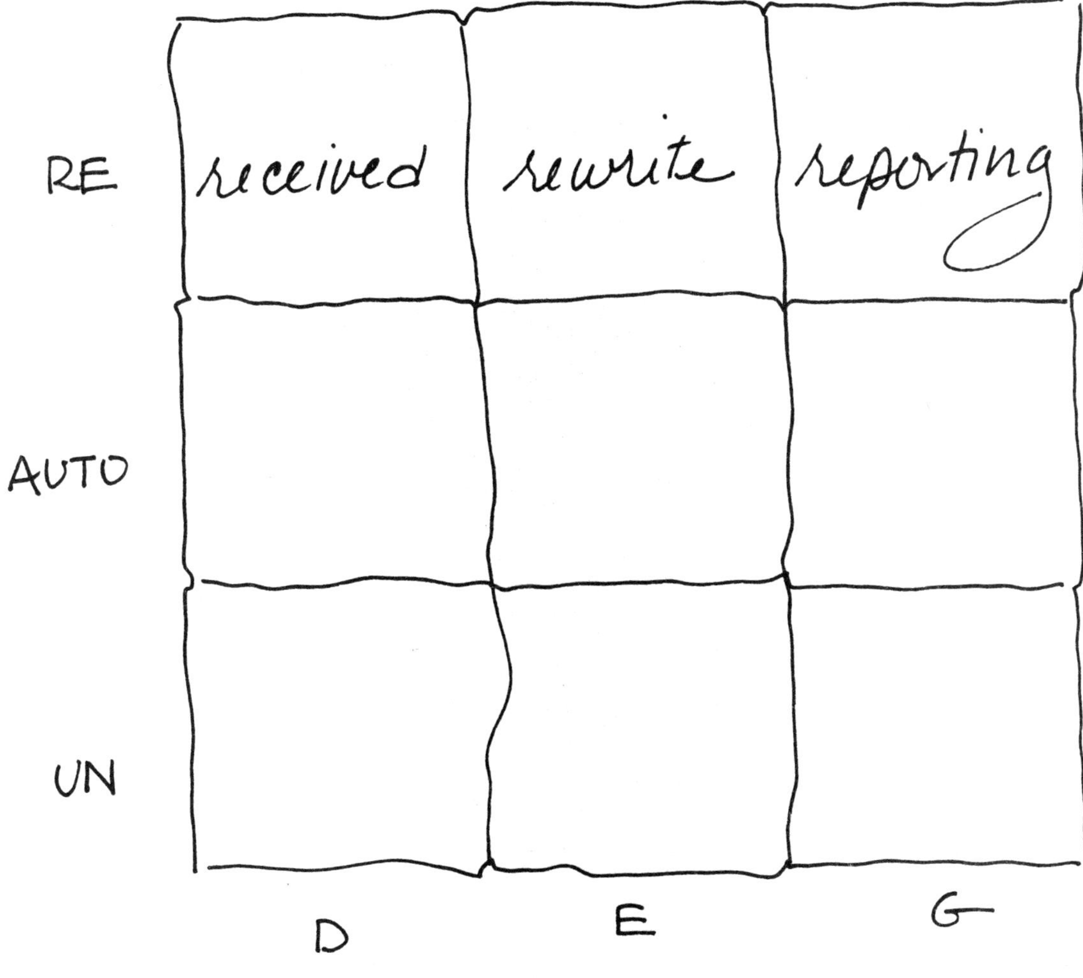

MORE...

Word Games

What are the longest words? Have the class create an ongoing list of long words.

What letters appear most frequently in words? Conduct an ongoing experiment. Conclude that "e" is the most common letter and that "t" is the most common initial letter.

What words are new to the English language? Which old words or phrases have taken on a new meaning? The list may include compact disc, hacker, user-friendly, bar code, yuppie.

What words sound the most beautiful when they are said? Ask students to write, then compare their choices.

What words both begin and end with the same letter? Choices may include arena, edge, gang, hearth.

What words begin and end with consecutive letters? Choices may include card, date, elf, frog, growth.

What words have the same letter occurring twice, but not together and not at the beginning or the end. Choices may include engage, meter, thighs, civil.

What words with five or more letters use only the first or second half of the alphabet? Choices may include blade, rusty, worst.

What words have the vowels a, e, i, o, u appear only once? What about unsociable?

What sentences can students write in which every word begins with the same letter?

Play "Plus One" in which each consecutive word uses the letters of the previous word, plus one more. For example, he.....she.....hers.....share.....hearts.....shatter.....

Play "Words in Words" in which students write words that can be spelled using the letters in a given word. For example, material: meat, team, tile, alarm, area.

Play "Wordmaker" in which a seven-letter word is chosen, such as "reading." The wordmaker writes a three-letter word on the chalkboard as a clue. The clue word consists of letters in any order taken from "reading," for example, "rid." Then students take turns writing words on the board to guess the wordmaker's word. If the word is not discovered, a four-letter clue word is written, such as "grin." Guessing continues. Finally a five-letter clue word, such as "grade." And so goes the game until the wordmaker's word is discovered.

Play "Anagrams" in which a word or phrase forms another word or phrase when the letters are rearranged. For example, "no" is an anagram for "on." Could your students figure these out?

they see......the eyes	two plus eleven...one plus twelve
life's aim....families	legislation.......Is it legal? No.
tender names..endearments	punishment........nine thumps
pittance......a cent tip	waitress..........A stew, sir?
one is apart..separation	astronomer........moon-starer

(from *Guinness Book of Words*, Martin Manser, Guinness, 1988)

MORE...

Cloze Connections

Prepare for the game by writing your own cloze material (selected letters, words, or phrases left blank for students to fill in) or use material already written. For an example of the latter, select a poem to read to the students. Write the poem leaving blanks for several high-use words. Then ask the students to write the missing words. This works well with short literature pieces and paragraphs of expository material. The activity is particularly effective for providing practice with homophones and other words that are often confused (then/than, are/our). It also works well to provide practice for unaccented vowels in words, such as en__my, hundr__d, poss__ble, beaut__ful. Some students may be able to create their own cloze games for other students to complete.

Word Sorts

Words can be sorted in many different ways. Methods of sorting words include meaning, number of letters, number of syllables, and by vowel sound or spelling. Prepare for the game by doing word sorting activities on the chalkboard. Then ask students to independently sort a set of words in some way. Select students to write their sorted words on the chalkboard. Then ask the class to determine how the words were sorted.

Word Suns

Draw a sunshine on the chalkboard or create one from construction paper for a bulletin board. Each ray of the sun represents one activity that can be done with a spelling word selected from the Core Word list. Identify the spelling word for the Word Suns game, then identify the activities. If the word selected is "record," the activities may include:

1. other words containing a /k/ sound spelled with a "c"
2. other words containing "or"
3. other words that begin with the prefix "re"
4. other word forms of "record"
5. other homographs (read, tear, object)

These activities can be done independently, then a class list of words for each activity can be recorded on the chalkboard.

Analogy Fun

Prepare students for analogous thinking by writing analogies on the chalkboard, such as "big is to little as up is to ________." If necessary, provide a bank of possible answers and complete the analogies together. Then have students independently complete blackline teacher-made analogies. Next, introduce the format "big : little:: up: _____." Challenge some students to write their own analogies for classmates to complete.

Visual Skill-Builders

See Build Visual Skills for a variety of game ideas that develop the visual modality (pages 113-115).

What about the students who do not readily make mind pictures—they cannot see a word and its individual letters when they close their eyes? The ability to use visual skills can be learned. The following activities provide opportunities for developing the skills of creating pictures in the mind. If used regularly, students will improve their personal visual imagery techniques. For spelling, this ability can significantly increase growth.

Immediate Recall

Provide opportunities for students to study and then recall the details of familiar things. For instance, show students the cover of a book, a simple picture, a display of common objects, or ask students to observe a classmate. Allow them a few moments to observe and think. Ask students to look at color, size, and shape. After removing the object(s) being studied, ask students to recall with visual pictures what they saw. Write, discuss, or draw the details remembered. Then compare the mental images with the actual thing.

Recall of Familiar Things

Provide opportunities for students to recall the details of familiar things they have seen in the past. For instance, ask students to create a mind picture of the school office, the principal, their kitchen at home, a paper clip, or a familiar object they often use and see. Write, discuss, or draw the details remembered. Then compare the mental images with the actual thing.

Developing Original Images

Provide opportunities for students to create mental pictures of something they have never seen. For instance, read students an unfamiliar story in which there is abundant action and descriptive scenes and characters. Stop the reading periodically to discuss the visions various students are creating in their minds. At some point in the story, stop and ask students to visualize and predict what might happen next. After reading the story, ask students to work in pairs to recreate through discussion,writing, or drawing selected parts of the story. As students read independently, remind them to picture in their minds what is taking place.

MORE...

Students need to develop the ability to see words differently for spelling and proofreading than they do for reading. Visual activities help the students to do this. Choose among these activities to build visual skills with each set of words taught:

GRID ACTIVITIES

Using a grid provided in the blackline master section of this handbook or graphing paper, ask the students to write their spelling words in the boxes. Students should extend the tall letters into the row of boxes above the base of the word. The "tail" letters should extend into the row of boxes below the base of the word. Then students can outline the word to call attention to its shape.

Word shapes can be drawn on the grid paper. Then students can write the appropriate word in each shape. These are called word shape, or configuration, activities.

The grids can be used for word search activities. Students can create their own word searches for a friend to complete. Any word in a word search should be written left-to-right and top-to-bottom.

Crossword puzzles lend themselves to the grids. Have students create their own for a friend to complete. Or give the students the crossword word clues...then they determine the words and create the puzzle around them.

With each of the grid activities, have the students write the word in the grid. Then turn the paper over, call the word up in their mind's eye, and write the word again. This incorporates the independent word-study procedure into each of these activities making the activities stronger ones.

WORDS IN WORDS

Students need to learn to direct their attention to the inside of words for effective spelling and proofreading of the words. Have students practice this by finding and writing words inside of their spelling words.

HIDDEN WORDS

Create a sequence of random letters in which the spelling words are written. Then have the students find and circle their spelling words. After they circle each word, ask the students to turn the paper over, call the word up in their mind's eye, and write the word.

MORE...

LOOK-ALIKE WORDS

Develop visual discrimination skills by creating a sequence of real words in a row that look very much like a spelling word that is a part of that sequence. For example: sheep street sleep peels sheet slip cheap

The spelling word is "sleep." The students must find and circle their spelling word. After they circle the spelling words in each row, ask the students to turn the paper over, call the spelling word up in their mind's eye, and write the word.

MEMORY, OR MNEMONIC, DEVICES

Ask students to create spelling clues for difficult words. For example, to discriminate between piece/peace, remember "piece of pie." The letters "pie" in each of the words create a memory device for using and spelling the correct word. Others may include "forty forts" or "the principal is your pal."

SCRAMBLES

The traditional spelling scramble asked students to rearrange the letters in a nonword to make a real word, one of their spelling words. However, there is often some risk in using nonwords in spelling activities. Students might interpret them as real words that are misspelled. Instead of using nonwords in scrambles, "float" the letters to be made into a word inside of a cloud shape. This format avoids any possible confusion. Again, as in each of the preceding activities, have the students rewrite the words on the back of their paper to incorporate the independent word-study procedure into the activity.

SOMETHING TO AVOID

...And here is an activity to AVOID...It often creates visual confusion that results in misspellings.

Many spelling books over the years have used sound-spelling activities for practice. These are sometimes called respelling activities or dictionary-spelling activities. The dictionary pronunciation of the word is written. Then the students write the regular spelling of the word (sum/some). Because spelling is a highly visual activity, the research indicates that it is unwise to use misspellings in spelling exercises.

A growing network of educators use Rebecca Sitton's SPELLING SOURCEBOOK methodology. Contact them for their opinions and advice. Following are just a few...call Rebecca for other users in your area. If you, too, would like your results included in seminar handbook updates, contact Rebecca. As many as possible will always be included to expand the options for informal information for educators interested in spelling literacy for their students.

The Loudoun County Public Schools report that their Iowa Test of Basic Skills scores increased in spelling with use of the SOURCEBOOK as their spelling foundation. **Betty Mar Little**, Instructional Supervisor, has been monitoring the increases, but warns that increased Iowa scores is *not* the "goal" of the district, but one of the significant outcomes associated with the SOURCEBOOK implementation. Contact her at 102 North Street NE, **Leesburg, VA** 22075 or 703-771-6400.∞∞∞∞∞∞∞∞Wausau, Wisconsin has successfully implemented the SOURCEBOOK approach to spelling literacy. **Greg Venne** (715-675-3351) handled the adoption of the materials and the pilots and **Nancy Caskey** (715-261-2537), the Director of Elementary Curriculum, is now guiding progress in grades 1-8. They report excellent improvement with good support from their School Board. Write to either of them at 1200 West Wausau Avenue in **Wausau, WI** 55401.∞∞∞∞∞∞∞∞Contact **Glenda Buck**, the Elementary Curriculum Supervisor, for information on the expansion of the program in Taylor School District outside Detroit. The district's address is 9551 Westlake, **Taylor, MI** 48180 and the phone is 313-295-5734. Teachers have put together a 2-hour parent meeting using the "Introduction to Parents" Video Tape Program. Middle school educators have asked to be included in this approach to spelling to use with their teams this year. ∞∞∞∞∞∞∞∞The Greenwich Public Schools have several exemplary teachers who use the SOURCEBOOKS as their spelling foundation. Contact the Director of Curriculum, **Faye Gage**, for a list of these teachers. She may be reached at 290 Greenwich Avenue, **Greenwich, CT** 06830 or 203-587-2580.∞∞∞∞∞∞∞∞**Kathleen Muzevich** is working with teachers to show objectively what their subjective evaluations reflect—a new spelling conscientiousness among 1-6 students in all their writing. Contact her in Governor Mifflin School District, 10 South Waverly Street, **Shillington, PA** 19607 or 610-775-5083.∞∞∞∞∞∞∞∞**Brenda Page** started the program after hearing about it in a seminar. It spread to her colleagues in grades 1-5 (they're moving it up to 6th grade

MORE....

this year) at Wakeeny Elementary in **Wakeeny, KS**. Then when her husband was transferred to central Kansas, she said she was lucky enough to find a job at another school who also used the SOURCEBOOKS. This year you'll find her at Westmoreland Elementary, Box 350, **Westmoreland, KS** 66549 or 913-457-3462. Ask her about her idea of inviting last year's parents to provide testimonials for their child's spelling progress to each new group of parents at her Fall Parent Night. Of course, this idea may be a little more difficult for her to do this year at her new school!∞∞∞∞∞∞∞Manzanita School, a Blue Ribbon School Winner awarded by the U. S. Department of Education, were disappointed with the results of their spelling instruction using traditional workbooks. After the first year of implementation of the SOURCEBOOK methodology, they report increased accuracy of spelling in writing. Teachers, students, and parents agree that the program's expectations for spelling high-use words correctly in writing has positively impacted students' everyday writing. Contact the principal, **Elizabeth Goettl**, at Manzanita for documentation for their school-wide spelling study, 3000 East Manzanita Avenue, **Tucson, AZ** 85718 or 602-577-5320.∞∞∞∞∞∞∞**Cindy Luna** is the principal at Howsman Elementary in Northside School District where **Shari Chu** teaches second grade. Read about Shari's exemplary SPELLING SOURCEBOOK classroom in LEARNING magazine (September 1995). Contact them at 11431 Vance Jackson, **San Antonio, TX** 78238 or 210-561-5040. **Dr. Kathleen Jongsma** is the Curriculum Director for this school district. She reports that district schools are showing progress with this approach to spelling. Contact her at 5900 Evers Road, San Antonio, TX 78238 or 210-706-8658.∞∞∞∞∞∞∞**Sharon Althouse** moved from Intermediate Education Unit 13 to the Language Arts Curriculum Director's position in Annville-Cleona School District last year. At Unit 13 she sponsored several training seminars for the SOURCEBOOK methodology and watched the excitement about students' spelling grow among teachers throughout the area. She is working on assessments now to show student spelling progress in Annville-Cleona. Contact her at 520 White Oak Road, **Annville, PA** 17033 or 717-867-4131.∞∞∞∞∞∞∞When New Ulm School District implemented the program, teachers loved the common sense of it according to principal **Tonya Schuell**. Ask her about the progress the students exhibit in their everyday writing. You may contact her at 318 South Payne, **New Ulm, MN** 56073 or 507-359-8460.∞∞∞∞∞∞∞**Joe Taylor** (principal) and the teachers at Brooks Elementary (grades 3-5, 600 students) felt the spelling progress they made was amazing, but predictable given the skills-plus-accountability approach of the SOURCEBOOK methodology. Overall, they had a 46% school-wide increase in students' ability to spell the high-use words with accuracy in writing during the 1995-1996 school year! Educators and parents are overwhelmingly supportive and eager to maintain this achievement. Contact them to let them describe exactly how they did it at 750 Natalie Drive, **Windsor, CA** 95492 or 707-837-7717.∞∞∞∞∞∞∞**Kim Rost** and the Manson Northwest Webster Schools are immensely pleased with spelling progress and are moving the program beyond the elementary and middle schools into the high school English classes beginning with the freshman and sophomores. Contact her at 1601 15th Street, **Manson, IA** 50563 or 712-469-2202.∞∞∞∞∞∞∞Souderton Area Schools are in the process of carefully documenting spelling gains and will share their progress with you. Contact **Dr. Marion Dugan**, Director of Curriculum and Staff

Development, at 139 Harleysville Pike, **Souderton, PA** 18964 or 215-723-6061. They have been in the program since the 1995-1996 school year.∞∞∞∞∞∞∞**Christine Carter**, the Assistant Superintendent for Instruction for the Roseville City School District, says her teachers using the methodology would never consider reverting to student spelling books because they've found that everyday writing provides far more practice than the books were ever able to offer. Contact them at 1000 Darling Way, **Roseville, CA** 95678 or 916-786-5090.∞∞∞∞∞∞∞**Jessie Woodley**, Language Arts Supervisor, has 30 years experience in education and wants all teachers to appreciate the opportunities for spelling literacy the SOURCEBOOKS provide. She has never seen such fine spelling results in students' daily writing! Further, she says "Students actually love spelling!" Contact her in the Shreveport Schools at Box 32000, **Shreveport, LA** 71130 or 318-638-6364.∞∞∞∞∞∞∞**Carol Ann Garcia** is completing her dissertation on spelling, specifically focusing on the progress students make using the SOURCEBOOK methodology. It will soon be complete, but preliminary findings show that students with teachers using the SOURCEBOOK approach are better spellers than those who are not using the program. She says many behaviors are too difficult to measure, but are nonetheless observable and show positive growth. One example is students' new willingness to seek out correct spellings as they write. Contact her at Holly Area Schools, 111 College Street, **Holly, MI** 48442 or 810-620-9528.∞∞∞∞∞∞∞**Linda Halbert**, 3rd grade teacher at Centennial Elementary School, attended a seminar on the SOURCEBOOK methodology in February '96. She immediately implemented the ideas and saw significant results in students' daily writing before the end of the school year! Contact her or her principal, **Linda Forbes**, at 1315 Aspen Street, **Springfield, OR** 97477 or 503-744-6383.∞∞∞∞∞∞∞The Shelton Board of Education conducted a SOURCEBOOK pilot to determine how well students transferred high-use words to writing. The results indicated, among other highly positive outcomes, that all students (high, middle, and low ability) maintained a 90% accuracy for spelling Priority Words correctly in writing *without* the use of their reference. This research surprised and pleased all! Contact **Patricia Curran**, Language Arts Supervisor, for details at 124 Meadow Street, **Shelton, CT** 06484 or 203-924-1023, ext. 324.∞∞∞∞∞∞∞Contact **Bobbie Hunt**, Language Arts Curriculum Director, for the North East School District at 8961 Tesoro, **San Antonio, TX** 78217 or 210-804-7177 to be referred to specific schools and teachers who can visit with you. **Pamela Darling** is a first grade teacher in this district at Windcrest Elementary who creates a fine environment for developing early spelling literacy with her class using the SOURCEBOOK suggestions.∞∞∞∞∞∞∞**Carol Purvine** and **Sue Oleszczuk**, the two administrators at the K-6 Arroyo Verde Elementary in the Redlands School District, have great progress to report thanks to their teachers focusing on fundamental skill development and spelling accountability as suggested in the SOURCEBOOKS. Contact them at 7701 Church Street, **Highland, CA** 92346 or 909-307-5590.∞∞∞∞∞∞∞**Carol Colvin**, Elementary Curriculum Director in the Hurst-Euless-Bedford Schools, asked her teachers to research spelling, pilot, and develop a plan for creating spelling literacy. They did and chose the SOURCEBOOK methodology. After over a year of study, full implementation is for the 1996-1997 school year. It was Carol who first said, "That old Friday Test is no

MORE...

more than a *parlor game!*" Contact her at 1849 Central Drive, **Bedford, TX** 76022 or 817-283-4461.∞∞∞∞∞∞∞The Cicero School District No. 99 just outside Chicago chose the SOURCEBOOK approach to spelling literacy after considerable committee study. Ask **Mirjana Skruodys**, the Language Arts Supervisor, about their process and implementation. She may be reached at 5110 West 24th Street, **Cicero, IL** 60650 or 708-863-4856.∞∞∞∞∞∞∞**Tish Costello**, Director of Elementary Programs in Cedar Hill School District, has her 1-6 teachers making progress with their use of the program. Now she's moving the methodology to grades 7-8. All support the philosophy 100%. Contact her at 270 South Hwy 67, **Cedar Hill, TX** 75104 or 214-291-1581.∞∞∞∞∞∞∞ **Jill Doyle**, principal at Way School, has a staff of teachers and a strong parent support group that contribute to the success of the program in affluent Bloomfield Hills Schools outside Detroit. Contact her at 765 West Long Lake Rd., **Bloomfield Hills, MI** 48302 or 810-645-4750.∞∞∞∞∞∞∞∞Contact **Dr. Maribeth Arentsen**, Merrill School District's Reading Coordinator, for information on their implementation of the program in grades 1-6 with follow through at 7-8. She stresses the importance of regular meetings for principals and teachers to facilitate a successful implementation process, including follow-up sessions using the training videos. She may be reached at 1111 North Sales, **Merrill, WI** 54452 or 715-536-2373.∞∞∞∞∞∞∞∞The Evergreen School District did a massive study of *every published spelling program* and spelling research before they decided upon the SOURCEBOOK methodology to complement and balance their curriculum. Citizens groups were involved in the decision early on which offered a strong block of support. Contact **Gary Simundson** in the Curriculum and Staff Development Department to find out more about their adoption process and implementation. He can be reached at 13510 NE 28th St., **Vancouver, WA** 98669 or 360-604-4000, ex 4465.∞∞∞∞∞∞∞∞**Melissa O'Donnell** and her colleagues in grades 1-4 at George C. Baker Elementary use the SOURCEBOOK materials within a community that demands high academic expectations for its students. The parents strongly embrace the program, as do the teachers. They have seen significant results in students' writing and, as Melissa says, "Spelling is fun to teach now!" Contact her at 139 West Maple Avenue, **Moorestown, NJ** 08057 or 609-778-6630.∞∞∞∞∞∞∞∞**Lynne Greenwood**, Director of K-12 Curriculum for the Ogden School District, was in search of a new direction for her teachers when she attended a Bureau of Education and Research seminar that provided the missing pieces found in the SOURCEBOOK approach. The district teachers needed "strategies and skills." Contact her at 5320 South Adams Avenue, **Ogden, Utah** 84405 or 801-476-7870.∞∞∞∞∞∞∞∞**Jinx Moore**, principal at Skyline Elementary School, initially "tried out" the SOURCEBOOK program in one class. It is now being implemented school wide. She may be reached at 2505 West 32nd, **Sedalia, MO** 65301 or 816-826-8087.∞∞∞∞∞∞∞∞Nobody is forcing the teachers in the Tomah School District to use the SPELLING SOURCEBOOK program, according to **Nancy Berklund** the Curriculum Director. They've all discovered that it works! Contact her at 219 West Clifton, **Tomah, WI** 54660 or 608-374-7232.∞∞∞∞∞∞∞ The Ashgrove School is seeing positive gains in spelling. Students are spelling better in their writing throughout all their classes across the curriculum. Contact the principal, **Al McClelland**, at 212 North 5th West, **Riverton, WY** 82501 or 307-856-2626. ∞∞∞∞∞∞∞Enthusiastic attendance at a SPELLING SOURCEBOOK seminar provided

MORE...

confirmation of the increasing number of schools in South-Western City School District that choose to use this approach to spelling. **Carmel Jenkins**, Reading Coordinator, says the program just keeps expanding. Contact her at 2975 Kingston Avenue, **Grove City, OH** 43123 or 614-875-2318.∞∞∞∞∞∞**Jackie Williams**, mentor teacher, uses the program and helps others to use it effectively. They are extremely pleased with the results. She sees the success of the program related to teacher training and likes the training videos as a follow up to the training seminar. Contact her at Grant School, 8835 Swasey Drive, **Redding, CA** 96001 or 916-243-0561.∞∞∞∞∞∞**Laura Smith**, teacher at Eastgate Elementary School, uses the parent-teacher conference to gain total parent support. Parents and teachers believe students should spell words correctly in their writing and they feel that use of the Priority Words is key to achieving this. Contact her at 910 East 10th, **Kennewick, WA** 99336 or 509-736-2120. **Brenda Hane**, at Sunset View Elementary, 711 Center Parkway, **Kennewick, WA** 99336 or 509-736-2155, also sees the success of the program tied to the expectations both parents and teachers have for the Priority Words. There are no excuses...these words are always spelled correctly!∞∞∞∞∞∞**Emil Aznar** reports that students at his school were not making the transition from creative spelling to conventional spelling until the SOURCEBOOK methodology was implemented. Now his teachers report progress developing students' basic spelling skills in writing. Contact him at Mentone Elementary School, 1320 Crafton Avenue, **Mentone, CA** 92359 or 909-794-8610.∞∞∞∞∞∞**Susan Zoller**, Curriculum Director for Bellingham School District, brought the program with her from another district in which she implemented it. She recommends inservice focusing on the correct use of the program as a key for a successful implementation. Contact her at 1306 Dupont Street, **Bellingham, WA** 98225 or 360-676-6400.∞∞∞∞∞∞**Stan Miller**, principal at Gold Run Elementary School, says that the critical element of the SPELLING SOURCEBOOK program is that it provides for authentic assessment through writing. His teachers support this over the out-dated Friday Test approach to spelling evaluation. Contact him at his school at 470 Searls Avenue, **Nevada City, CA** 95959 or 916-265-1830.∞∞∞∞∞∞**Mimi Battle** works with teachers in the Eureka School District for successful implementation of the SOURCEBOOK methodology. For example, she helps them in setting up their Priority Word lists. Contact her at Grant Elementary School, 3901 G Street, **Eureka, CA** 95503 or 707-441-2552.∞∞∞∞∞∞**Gwen O'Banon** is creating a model for implementing the SPELLING SOURCEBOOK methodology through trained mentor teachers in her large school district. She feels on-site help through fully-trained mentor teachers is critical for the implementation of new programs. Contact her at Lewisville Independent School District, 247 West Main. **Lewisville, TX** 75057 or 214-219-6909.∞∞∞∞∞∞**Stacy Kaase** reports significant spelling growth for every one of her fifth graders with the use of the SOURCEBOOK methodology. This improvement is visible in her students' writing and on her CAT scores. CAT scores are <u>up</u>! Parents embraced the program 100% from the onset, saying it "makes sense." Let Stacy tell you how she does it—contact her at Taunton Forge Elementary School, 32 Evergreen Trail, **Medford, NJ** 08055 or 609-654-6723.

This appendix contains reproducible masters. The masters may be copied for classroom use.

How to Use Blackline Masters
Preview and Review Form
Blackline Example for Special Needs
Word Study Sheet
Grid (large squares)
Grid (small squares)

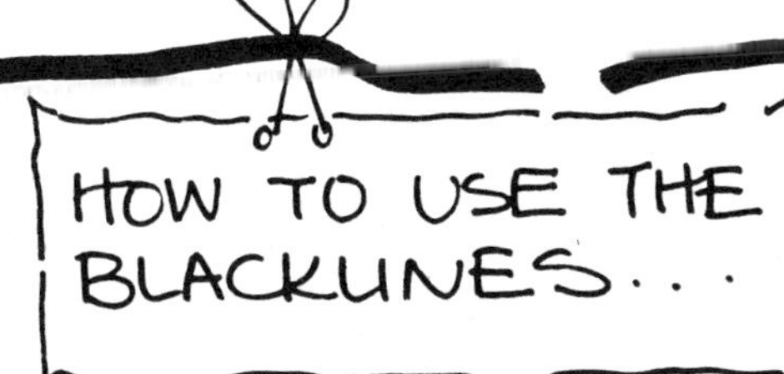

All the blackline masters may be reproduced for classroom use. They can be modified to better meet the needs of the students. For example, primary students may benefit from a master that has more space between writing lines with a dotted center line.

Preview and Review Master

Use this blackline for students as they take the Preview and the Review. Students print the word in the left column as it is dictated by the teacher. Students print the word in the right column from the teacher's model on the chalkboard (chart, overhead) during the self-correction procedure.

Blackline Master (Example for Special Needs)

This blackline is an example of a teacher-made blackline for use with students for whom the Preview-Review activity of Core Words is too challenging. The Core Words cannot be read by these students, so attempting to spell them would be inappropriate. Nonetheless, the teacher wants the students to participate in the procedure. They may do so by providing the students with a master with the words for use in the Preview-Review dotted in within the blanks for the "Write" column. When the word is said by the teacher for the class to spell, the students with this special blackline master trace the word by following the dots. When the class is writing the word in the "Rewrite" column, these students do so, too. However, their word model is the word they just traced in the "Write" column. This method serves as a reading and writing activity as well as a classroom management aid.

Word Study Master

Use this master for students to study any other words they need or want to learn. First, they look at the word to be learned on a model. They <u>read</u> this word from a model, <u>spell</u> the word (perhaps touching each letter with the point of their pencil as the word is spelled), <u>cover</u> the word so that it is not visible, <u>print</u> the word on the top line of the left-hand column, uncover the word and <u>proofread</u> the word against the model. Students should practice until they can print the word correctly two times in a row. If they do so in the first two columns, practice is complete.

The Grid Masters

The grid blacklines can be used for visual practice of words. Have students print their words in the boxes using two vertical boxes for tall or tail letters. Then have students outline the shape of the word. This is a configuration or word-shape activity. It helps students learn to visualize their spelling words and to picture each letter as a separate unit, rather than the way words are observed for reading. Students may also use the grids for creating word-search puzzles and crossword puzzles. Use the grid with the larger boxes for younger students and the one with smaller boxes for older students.

Write	Rewrite
1.	1.
2.	2.
3.	3.
4.	4.
5.	5.
6.	6.

Write	Rewrite
1 The	1
2 this	2

make a master
for special needs
students. See
page 122.

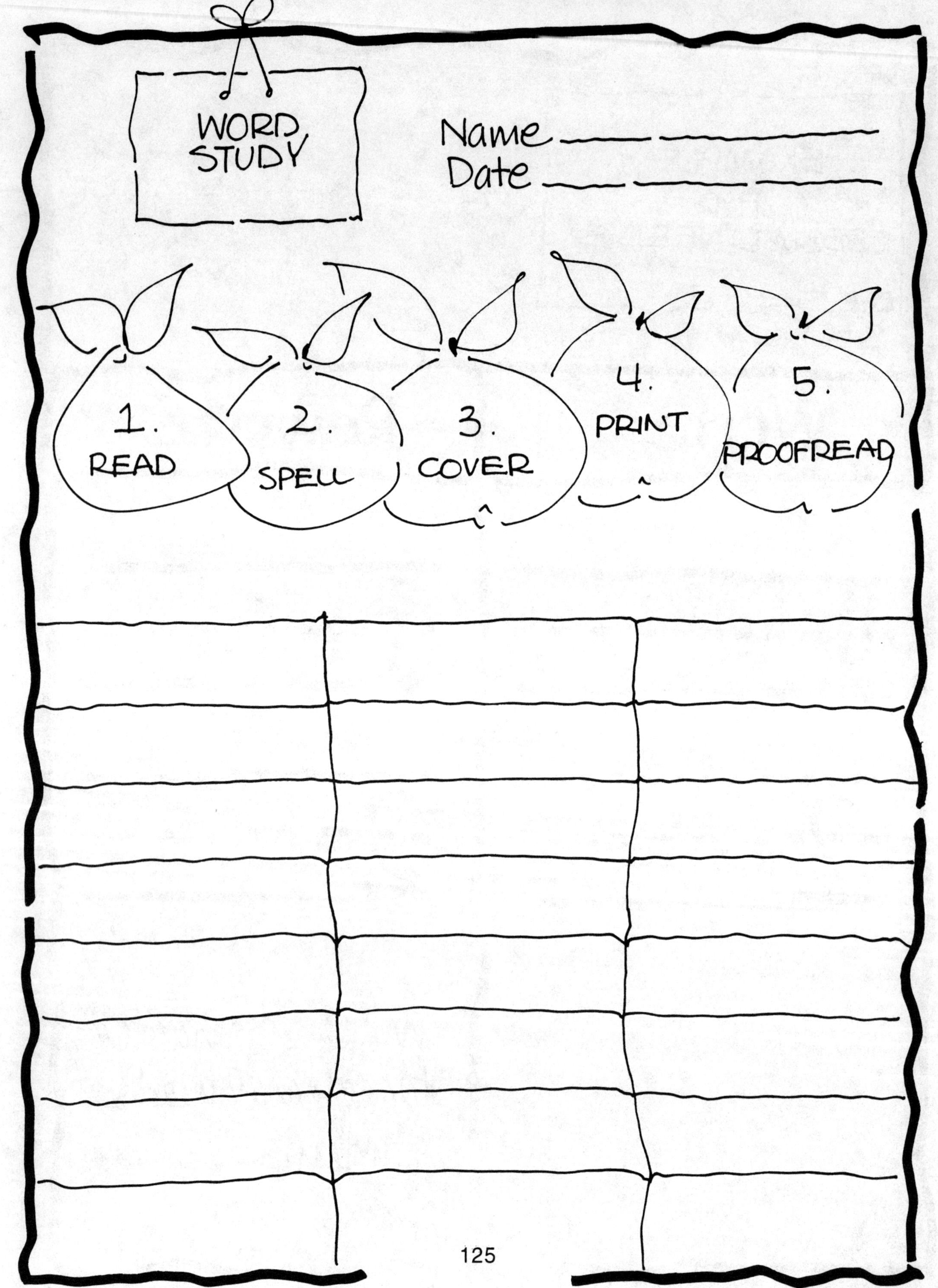

WORD STUDY
Name
Date
1.
READ
2.
SPELL
3.
COVER
4.
PRINT
5.
PROOFREAD

Name _______________________

Name_______________________

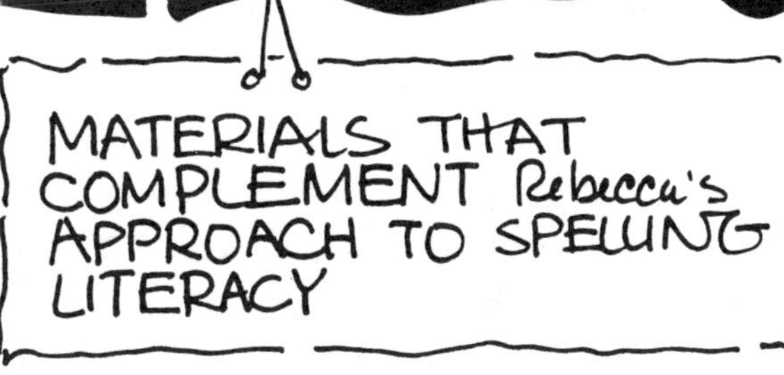

This materials section contains resources available for your use.

<u>The SPELLING SOURCEBOOK Series for Spelling and Language Literacy</u>
        SPELLING SOURCEBOOKS 1, 2, 3, and 4
        SPELLING SOURCEBOOK Training Videos
            Video Tape I: Introduction to Teachers
            Video Tape II: Introduction to Parents
            Video Tape III: Management & Record Keeping Options
            Video Series Training Guide for Staff Development
        SPELLING SOURCEBOOK Preview Video
        SPELLING SOURCEBOOK Reviews
            For High-Use Writing Words 1-400
            For High-Use Writing Words 401-800 (available this winter)
            For High-Use Writing Words 801-1200 (available spring, 1997)
        WORD-WISE SOURCEBOOKS: Laugh-Aloud Rhymes for Learning
            Language Skills
        SPELLING SOURCEBOOK Materials Order Form

<u>Materials That Complement Rebecca Sitton's SPELLING SOURCEBOOK Series</u>

        INCREASING STUDENT SPELLING ACHIEVEMENT
        AUDIO TAPE Series
        INSTANT SPELLING WORDS FOR WRITING
        INSTANT WORD EXPERIENCES
        THE SPELLING WORKSHOPS
        STOP AND THINK--THE LIFESKILLS LITERACY Series
        THE QUICK-WORD HANDBOOK FOR EVERYDAY WRITERS
        THE QUICK-WORD HANDBOOK FOR BEGINNING WRITERS
        THE QUICK-WORD HANDBOOK FOR PRACTICAL WRITING
        THE QUICK-WORD HANDBOOK FOR SPANISH WRITERS
        THE QUICK-WORD WORDSHOP Series
        VIDEO PROGRAM: WHAT WORKS? ACHIEVING SPELLING LITERACY in
            EVERYDAY WRITING

REBECCA SITTON'S <u>SPELLING SOURCEBOOK</u> SERIES
Northwest Textbook ✳ 503-639-3193
(See the order form in the back of this handbook. Orders are shipped within 24 hours after the order is received. Two-Day Delivery shipments are available for rush orders.)

The SPELLING SOURCEBOOK Series has grown as a result of teacher requests for resources to create their own writing-based spelling curriculum. The materials in the Series are listed, followed by a description of each:

- SPELLING SOURCEBOOKS 1, 2, 3, and 4
- SPELLING SOURCEBOOK Training Videos
    - Video Tape I: Introduction to Teachers
    - Video Tape II: Introduction to Parents
    - Video Tape III: Management & Record Keeping Options
    - Video Series Training Guide for Staff Development
- SPELLING SOURCEBOOK Preview Video
- SPELLING SOURCEBOOK Reviews
    - For High-Use Writing Words 1-400
    - For High-Use Writing Words 401-800 (available this winter)
    - For High-Use Writing Words 801-1200 (available spring, 1997)
- WORD-WISE SOURCEBOOKS: Laugh-Aloud Rhymes for Learning Language Skills

Description of the <u>SPELLING SOURCEBOOK</u> Materials

<u>SPELLING SOURCEBOOK 1</u>: Every teacher using the Series needs SPELLING SOURCEBOOK 1. This is the how-to book for developing, implementing, teaching day-to-day, and authentically assessing your custom-designed spelling curriculum. It contains multiple resources including the 1200 high-use writing words, practices supported and NOT supported by research, the valid spelling rules, multiple spelling games and activities, over 100 writing motivators, and blackline masters for practice procedures and record keeping.

<u>SPELLING SOURCEBOOK 2</u>: Teachers in grades 1-4 use this book in addition to SPELLING SOURCEBOOK 1. It contains the language-integrated activities for developing basic skills using high-use words 1-400.

<u>SPELLING SOURCEBOOK 3</u>: Teachers in grades 5-6 use this book in addition to SPELLING SOURCEBOOK 1. It contains the language-integrated activities for developing basic skills using high-use words 401-800.

<u>SPELLING SOURCEBOOK 4</u>: Teachers in grades 5-6 use this book in addition to SPELLING SOURCEBOOK 1. It contains the language-integrated activities for developing basic skills using high-use words 801-1200.

Teachers choose the SPELLING SOURCEBOOK activities they wish to do and skip the others—there are too many to do them all. Their choices are based on their teaching style, the needs of their students, their time frame, and their school's instructional guidelines. See activity samples on next page.

320 *space*

Book Tie-In, Writing a Journal Entry

A Flight of Discovery Aboard the Space Shuttle (Barbara Embury, Harper, 1990) uses dramatic pictures and text to describe what shuttle passengers see when they look back to Earth. Have students write a journal entry for one day in space aboard the shuttle.

Book Tie-In, Writing Predictions, Vocabulary Skills

For a dictionary of space vocabulary, use Space Words (Seymour Simon, HarperCollins, 1991). The dictionary format includes illustrations and concise explanations. Before exploring the book, have students list those words they think will be included.

Sound-Symbol Awareness, Writing Sentences

Ask students to write *space*. Then have them follow these directions to write new and review words:

Change *space* to make *face* (291), *race, grace, lace, place* (131).
Change *space* to make *spice*.
Change *space* to make *ace*.

Have students write a sentence for each word they made.

Other Word Forms, Vocabulary Skills, Writing Sentences

Have students brainstorm for common other word forms of *space: spaces, spaced, spacing, spacious.* Discuss unfamiliar words. Have students write the other word forms in sentences.

Research and Writing, Public Speaking

Have students research one of the following topics, tell about their findings in writing, and then present the information orally to the class:

Sally Ride
current NASA projects
the qualifications required of astronauts

1125 *disappear*

Other Word Forms, Writing Questions and Answers, Reasoning

Have students brainstorm for common other word forms of *disappear: disappears, disappeared, disappearing, disappearance.* Then ask students to write this question and the answer: How do magicians make objects appear to disappear?

Prefix Practice, Antonyms, Writing Sentences

Ask students to remove a prefix from *disappear* to make its antonym (*appear*). Then have them use a prefix to write the word that means "to appear again" (*reappear*). Have students write *appear, disappear,* and *reappear* in sentences.

Research and Writing, Drawing Conclusions, Book Tie-In

Have students research historical disappearances. Then have them draw written conclusions about their explanation. Topics and resources may include the dinosaurs, Why Did the Dinosaurs Disappear?: Questions About Life in the Past (Philip Whitfield, Viking, 1991); the Anasazi, The Ancient Cliff Dwellers of Mesa Verde (Caroline Arnold, Clarion, 1992); and Amelia Earhart, Amelia Earhart: Missing, Declared Dead (Anita Larsen, Crestwood, 1992).

Writing Speculations

What jobs have disappeared or diminished in the last fifty years? What jobs may be disappearing in the future? Which new jobs will take their place? Have students answer in writing.

Analyzing Meanings, Rewriting

Have students rewrite this sentence, replacing the metaphor with literal language: He's the magician's disappearing rabbit when there's work to be done.

Description of the <u>SPELLING SOURCEBOOK</u> Materials (Continued)

<u>VIDEO TAPE I</u>: Introduction to Teachers
This is a 70-minute teacher-training video highlighting the information covered in the first half of the full day seminar—a "must" for teachers new to the program and a fast-paced overview for experienced teachers needing a refresher.
<u>VIDEO TAPE II</u>: Introduction to Parents
This a a 40-minute parent introduction—a highly informative overview designed to quickly establish parent understanding and support.
<u>VIDEO TAPE III</u>: Management and Record Keeping Options
This is a 70-minute teacher-training video highlighting the information covered in the second half of the full-day seminar—a "must" for teachers new to the program or for those who need a refresher for understanding the differences between the Priority and Core Words, as well as easy management ideas.

<u>VIDEO SERIES Training Guide for Staff Development</u>:
This manual was developed by Christy Fong, master teacher-trainer. It complements the use of Videos I and III with structured mini-viewing sessions featuring questions, discussions, and activities to enhance learning. The guide includes the master for making a training booklet for each teacher participant.

<u>SPELLING SOURCEBOOK Preview Video</u>:
It's free! This 20-minute on-loan introduction to the SPELLING SOURCEBOOK approach to spelling and language literacy can be ordered by calling 509-534-1000. It's not a training video, but a quick overview of what this series is all about. Call now!

<u>SPELLING SOURCEBOOK Reviews</u>: Your Source for Blackline Master Cloze Activities and Sentence Dictation Sentences

For high-use writing words 1-400 (correlated to SOURCEBOOK 2)
For high-use writing words 401-800 (correlated to SOURCEBOOK 3)
For high-use writing words 801-1200 (correlated to SOURCEBOOK 4)
The Reviews have two purposes. They provide in-context <u>spelling practice</u> for students and a <u>spelling assessment</u> opportunity for teachers to note progress students are making toward word mastery in writing. There are 80 lessons in each book. The lessons have two parts: A blackline cloze story and a set of dictation sentences. Each lesson focuses on five Core Words sequentially in frequency-of-use order. They can be used to end a Core Word unit. The cloze story is read to the students as they follow along on their copy, writing the missing words in the blanks. Words that have been the most persistently misspelled and misused by writers are reviewed again and again in the cloze stories. Each cloze story is followed by a set of activities that send the students back into the story for further growth on topics including homophones, words with multiple meanings, phonics, synonyms, and word sorting exercises. Each set of dictation sentences features a thinking-writing follow-up activity related to the topic developed within the sentences.

Description of the <u>SPELLING SOURCEBOOK</u> Materials (Continued)

<u>WORD-WISE SOURCEBOOKS:</u>   Laugh-Aloud   Rhymes   for   Learning <u>Language Skills</u>

Get ready! Dr. Barbara Schmidt and Dr. Maurice Poe will have your students laughing and learning with their three NEW books of word-wise rhymes and activities! You'll be laughing right along with them!

There are three WORD-WISE SOURCEBOOKS—one for grades one and two, another for grades three and four, and the third for grades five and six. All poems are on <u>blackline masters</u> so each student can have a copy! Make a child-centered take-home book of the poems! All poems have multiple motivational follow-up activities to help students become WORD WISE.

Here's a rhyme that opens an exciting set of synonym activities for young writers—

Say It Better

Throw out "big," it's just too boring.
"Said" puts me to sleep and snoring.
Some words are old, throw them away.
Let's think up better words today.

Instead of "big," think "huge" or "wide,"
Instead of "said," think "shouted," "cried."
Instead of "little," try for "tiny,"
Use words that sparkle new and shiny!

In this poem, Wordy Birdy introduces color words to young writers...then students write their own rhymes—

Color Me Pink

Wordy fell into the bathtub.
Wordy fell into the sink.
Wordy fell into the cherry jam
And came out PINK!

Wordy fell into the bucket.
Wordy fell into the bed.
Wordy fell into the berry jam
And came out RED!

And now the students try it...

I fell into a big box.
I fell into the stew.
I fell into the berry jam
And came out ________.

132

Materials That Complement
Rebecca Sitton's SPELLING SOURCEBOOK Series

<u>INCREASING STUDENT SPELLING ACHIEVEMENT</u>
Northwest Textbook ✳ *503-639-3193*
(See the order form in the back of this handbook)
This is <u>this</u> seminar handbook. For information on scheduling a seminar for your school or school district, call Rebecca Sitton at 509-535-5500 or Egger Publishing, Inc. at 509-534-1000.

<u>AUDIO TAPE PROGRAM: INCREASING STUDENT SPELLING ACHIEVEMENT</u>
Bureau of Education and Research ✳ *1-800-735-3503*
This audio program is Rebecca's full-day INCREASING STUDENT SPELLING ACHIEVEMENT seminar taped live in Madison, Wisconsin.

<u>INSTANT SPELLING WORDS FOR WRITING</u>
<u>(Teacher Guides and Student Books)</u>
Rebecca Sitton and Dr. Robert Forest
Curriculum Associates, Inc. ✳ *1-800-225-0248*
This eight-level research-based series is an alternative to traditional basal spelling. It teaches the high-use words in the order of their frequency of use. There are extensive language-integrated ideas...an emphasis on visual skills...easy to follow directions. Use this series with students who would benefit from additional spelling practice.

<u>INSTANT WORD EXPERIENCES</u>
Rebecca Sitton and Dr. Robert Forest
Curriculum Associates, Inc. ✳ *1-800-225-0248*
This new literature-based program provides all the developmentally appropriate experiences beginning writers (K-1) need prior to formal spelling instruction. Multiple experiences with the high-use writing words unfold from folktale favorites. No spelling tests, but lots of non-threatening, motivational, language-rich activities.

<u>THE SPELLING WORKSHOPS correlated to HEATH INTEGRATED READING</u>
Rebecca Sitton
DC Heath ✳ *1-800-235-3565*
This is a spelling program that is specifically correlated to the literature in Heath's Integrated Reading.

<u>STOP AND THINK—THE LIFESKILLS LITERACY SERIES</u>
Rebecca Sitton and Kathleen Schaefer
Curriculum Associates, Inc. ✳ *1-800-225-0248*
This is an extremely popular, cost-effective series for older learners needing spelling and language experiences, as well as critical lifeskills information. The centerpiece of each of the three titles is a lifeskill topic: using credit cards, finding a job, buying a car.

<u>THE QUICK-WORD HANDBOOK SERIES</u>
Rebecca Sitton and Dr. Robert Forest
Curriculum Associates, Inc. ✳ *1-800-225-0248*

Why are the QUICK-WORD HANDBOOKS the most popular spelling reference guides in American and Canadian schools? They're cost-effective..easy for kids to use...and they use them! **Call Curriculum Associates for a free sample!**

<u>THE QUICK-WORD HANDBOOK FOR EVERYDAY WRITERS</u>: Use this yellow QUICK-WORD in grades 2 or 3 through 8. It lists the 1020 highest-frequency writing words, provides space for a student's own special words, clarifies homophones, and provides a reference for states, numbers, months, days, and common abbreviations. Use the pink CANADIAN QUICK-WORD for developing Canadian spellers and writers.

<u>THE QUICK-WORD HANDBOOK FOR BEGINNING WRITERS</u>: Use this lavender QUICK-WORD for K-1 students. Some grade 2 teachers may prefer this QUICK-WORD. This developmentally appropriate QUICK-WORD gets young writers off to a comfortable start with spelling.

<u>THE QUICK-WORD HANDBOOK FOR PRACTICAL WRITING</u>: Use this aqua QUICK-WORD for more mature writers in high school or adult education who may feel uncomfortable with a large dictionary. It includes survival words, such as "No Trespassing," a feature which will help students for whom English is a second language.

<u>THE QUICK-WORD HANDBOOKS FOR SPANISH WRITERS</u>: These two QUICK-WORDS, one for primary and one for intermediate learners, provide a spelling resource for Spanish words.

<u>THE QUICK-WORD WORDSHOP SERIES</u>
Rebecca Sitton
Curriculum Associates, Inc. ✳ *1-800-225-0248*

You asked for it! Not a spelling book, but a thematic language-integrated activity series that ensures extra practice-in-context of the high-frequency writing words found in students' QUICK-WORD HANDBOOKS. The ungraded booklets are appropriate for students in grades 3-8. There are four QUICK-WORD WORDSHOP titles:

<u>FLIGHT</u>: eagles, Sally Ride, kites, hot-air balloons, etc.
<u>BIG IDEAS</u>: huge roller coasters, Great Wall of China, etc.
<u>WEIRD WONDERS</u>: why popcorn pops, number tricks, quicksand, etc.
<u>OUR AMERICA</u>: National Park System, Statue of Liberty, etc.

<u>VIDEO PROGRAM: WHAT WORKS? ACHIEVING SPELLING LITERACY in EVERYDAY WRITING</u>

NEW!

Satellite Communications Educational Programming ✳ *509-536-2172*

This live one-hour broadcast of Rebecca Sitton discussing spelling is available on video. The fast-paced instructional program introduces the SPELLING SOURCEBOOK methodology. Ask for Katie Kuetemeyer.

SPELLING SOURCEBOOK 1
Northwest Textbook, (503-639-3193)
This is your source for how to develop your own program, implement it, teach it day-to-day, and assess student progress. Every teacher using the SOURCEBOOK methodology needs a personal copy of this manual. It includes everything an educator needs for knowing how to use Rebecca Sitton's approach to spelling literacy.

SPELLING SOURCEBOOK VIDEOS
Northwest Textbook, (503-639-3193)
There are two training videos that explain the SPELLING SOURCEBOOK methodology to teachers.

Tape I— **Introduction to Teachers:** A 70-minute introduction that highlights information in the first half of the full-day training seminar

Tape III— **Management & Record Keeping Options:** A 70-minute follow-up to Tape I expanding the training to grading, record keeping, and organizing the program

SPELLING SOURCEBOOK VIDEO SERIES TRAINING GUIDE FOR STAFF DEVELOPMENT
Northwest Textbook, (503-639-3193)
This guidebook is the step-by-step partner for the teacher trainer using the SPELLING SOURCEBOOK VIDEOS. It expands the video training to mini-sessions of activities and discussion that follow video training segments.

AUDIO TAPE SEMINAR "Increasing Student Spelling Achievement"
Bureau of Education and Research, (800-735-3503)
This multi-tape program is one version of Rebecca's Bureau of Education and Research seminar.

VIDEO PROGRAM: WHAT WORKS? ACHIEVING SPELLING LITERACY IN EVERYDAY WRITING
Satellite Communications Educational Programming, (509-536-2172)
This one-hour overview of the SOURCEBOOK methodology highlights key elements of the program recorded live on a satellite educational network, Spring '96.

LIVE TRAINING SEMINAR TAILORED TO YOUR NEEDS
Egger Publishing, Inc., (509-534-1000)
Rebecca Sitton and her associates Christy Fong and Barbara Hanno train thousands of teachers every year to successfully implement the SPELLING SOURCEBOOK methodology. This training can be scheduled for one school, a group of schools, a school district, several districts, a county office of education or any regional education agency...any group size.

ORDER FORM

Description	Qty.	Price	Total
Increasing Student Spelling Achievement			
Spelling Seminar Handbook 1 – 49 copies	____	$15.00	$________
50 or more	____	$ 9.00	$________

SOURCEBOOKS

Description		Qty.	Price	Total
Spelling Sourcebook™ 1	1 – 49 copies	____	$26.50	$________
	50 or more*	____	$21.50	$________
Spelling Sourcebook™ 2	1 – 49 copies	____	$26.50	$________
	50 or more*	____	$21.50	$________
Spelling Sourcebook™ 3	1 – 49 copies	____	$26.50	$________
	50 or more*	____	$21.50	$________
Spelling Sourcebook™ 4	1 – 49 copies	____	$26.50	$________
	50 or more*	____	$21.50	$________

* Any combination of Sourcebooks 1, 2, 3 or 4 totaling 50 copies or more

VIDEO TRAINING TAPES

Description	Qty.	Price	Total
Tape I Introduction to Teachers	____	$150.00	$________
Tape II Introduction to Parents	____	$100.00	$________
Tape III Management and Record Keeping Options	____	$150.00	$________
Video Series Training Guide for Staff Development	____	$30.00	$________
Tape Set (one of each tape)	____	$350.00	$________
Tape Set WITH Training Guide	____	$380.00	$________

> For special video broadcast and duplication rights, contact Egger Publishing, Inc.

SPELLING SOURCEBOOK™ REVIEWS

Description	Qty.	Price	Total
For High-Use Writing Words 1 – 400	____	$38.50	$________
For High-Use Writing Words 401 – 800 Available Fall '96	____	$38.50	$________
For High-Use Writing Words 801 – 1200 Available Winter '96	____	$38.50	$________

WORD-WISE SOURCEBOOKS™

Description	Qty.	Price	Total
Level 1, for Grades 1 and 2 Available July '96	____	$42.50	$________
Level 2, for Grades 3 and 4 Available Fall '96	____	$42.50	$________
Level 3, for Grades 5 and 6 Available Fall '96	____	$42.50	$________

MERCHANDISE TOTAL	$________
ADD TAX: 8.25% in CA; 8.1% in WA	$________
ADD POSTAGE & HANDLING:	$________

	U.S.	CANADA	
$0 – 499	8%	14%	$4 min. U.S.
$500 – 999	$40.00	$70.00	$8 min. Canada
$1000 and up	4%	7%	

TOTAL ORDER	$________

Canadian orders must be paid in U.S. funds (Canadian shipments are subject to customs/brokerage/GST fees to be paid on delivery) • *Prices subject to change without notice*

BILL TO:

District ____________________

Att'n: ____________________

Address ____________________

City ____________ State ____

Zip ____________________

Phone ____________________

Fax ____________________

SHIP TO:

Name ____________________

School ____________________

Address ____________________

City ____________ State ____

Zip ____________________

Phone ____________________

Fax ____________________

CHOOSE YOUR PAYMENT METHOD:

☐ Bill school / district:
Purchase order no. ____________

Personal orders:

☐ Check

☐ VISA

☐ MasterCard

Expiration date ☐☐ - ☐☐

Card Account No.

☐☐☐☐☐☐☐☐☐☐☐☐☐☐☐☐

Authorized Signature

____

Does this confirm an order already submitted by phone or fax? ____________

Here's where to send your order:

Northwest Textbook
17970 SW McEwan Rd.
Portland, OR 97224
(503) 639-3193
fax: (503) 639-2559

Questions? Contact:

Egger Publishing, Inc.
P.O. Box 4466
Spokane, WA 99202
(509) 534-1000
fax: (509) 534-6971